COSORI
AIR FRYER
COOKBOOK FOR
BEGINNERS
UK 🇬🇧 2023

Delicious, Quick & Foolproof COSORI Air Fryer
Recipes for Your Whole Family and Friends

Susan Hoffman

Table of Content

Chapter 5 Poultry   30

Chapter 6 Snacks and Appetizers   39

Chapter 7 Fish and Seafood   47

Chapter 8 Desserts   55

INTRODUCTION

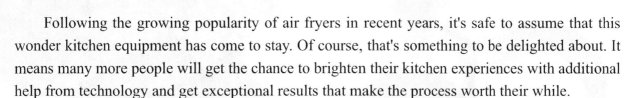

Following the growing popularity of air fryers in recent years, it's safe to assume that this wonder kitchen equipment has come to stay. Of course, that's something to be delighted about. It means many more people will get the chance to brighten their kitchen experiences with additional help from technology and get exceptional results that make the process worth their while.

However, with growing popularity comes the proliferation of brands trying to meet market demands. There are now so many air fryer brands out there that choosing one for your kitchen can in itself be an arduous task. When I decided to get an air fryer, I had to extensively research various air fryer brands before settling for one that perfectly meets my requirements.

If like me, you want to bring more functionality into your kitchen, discover new ways to make your choice recipes, and explore new worlds of recipes, then you should absolutely give the Cosori Air Fryer a try. Do you hate cooking? Maybe because it can be messy sometimes or it takes too much time. Your hatred may stem from your inability to get cooking results similar to those you see in your favorite cookbooks. A Cosori air fryer might just be the thing to turn your story around as it did for a friend who has been happily cooking multiple times daily since she purchased one recently.

However, choosing the right air fryer, Cosori of course, is only the first step towards that transformation you seek for your experience in the kitchen. You can only get the best out of all the functionality the Cosori air fryer offers with the right repertoire of cuisines and recipes and that's what this cookbook brings to you.

In the following pages, I have assembled a wide collection of recipes from different cultures to stimulate your creativity in the kitchen and inspire you to explore a totally new world of tasty and savoury dishes as you get started with your Cosori air fryer. Whether this is your first time using an air fryer or you're a veteran changing gears, there's a recipe for you in here.

A significant number of the recipes use easy-to-get everyday ingredients, so you won't have to endure additional stress looking for ingredients. And the instructions are written in simple and plain language, with easy-to-follow steps.

Let's get on this journey already. I hope you enjoy every bit of it and get outstanding results.

Chapter 1 Cosori Air Fryer Basic Guide

Chapter 1 Cosori Air Fryer Basic Guide

Cosori air fryers are one of the world's leading air fryer brands. It originates from Southern California where it was first launched in 2018. With over 94,000 reviews and a rating of 4.7 stars, the Cosori air fryer is arguably one of the most popular air fryer brands on the market today.

These air fryers follow the dominant drawer model common amongst the leading brands. Hence, it typically comprises of two basic parts: they air fryer itself and the baskets. The baskets, though usually locked in together, can be separated into the inner and the outer baskets.

One of the unique attributes of the Cosori range of air fryers is its compact design. They won't require enormous space on your shelf, yet, thanks to its squarish basket design, you can make use of every possible space available for your cooking.

Cosori air fryers are also functionally smart and aesthetically pleasing. No matter what model you go for, you can be sure it will improve the general outlook of your kitchen

How Does Cosori Air Fryer Work?

The Cosori air fryer uses a heating process called convection. This process involves the transfer of heat via a heated fluid medium, which, in this case, is air. Unlike the deep-frying process, which conveys heat through oil, it can give your food just as much browning and crispiness as deep-frying, if not more.

These air fryers include two square-shaped baskets: the inner and the outer basket. The inner basket has vents on all sides, allowing free hot air circulation around the food. The inner basket goes into the outside basket, where it is suspended to aid air circulation and the collection of excess liquid from your food, ensuring that you consume minimal fat.

5 Basic Features of Cosori Air Fryers

Cosori air fryers possess the following features, which make them a leading brand in the market:

Auto Pause and Resume

Want to take a peep at what you're cooking? No problem. The Cosori air fryer automatically pauses cooking when you pull out the baskets. And you wouldn't have to worry about your safety as the display also turns off temporarily. As soon as you push the baskets back in, the air fryer resumes cooking based on your previous settings.

Large Capacity

Cosori air fryers are designed to give you the maximum space possible for your cooking. Depending on the model you go for, the baskets come in varying capacities, from 5 quartz and above. Furthermore, the manufacturers use a square shape design to provide more cooking capacity and flexibility than round designs. With a typical Cosori air fryer, you can cook enough food for a family of 3-5 at once.

Automatic Shutoff

Air fryers generally require less power to function, and they cook food about 30% faster than regular ovens. Cosori air fryers can help you save even more energy with their automatic shutoff function. This function kicks in after three minutes of inactivity on the fryer. The appliance will clear all settings and turn itself off. So even if you get distracted and forget that the

machine is turned on, you can rest assured that it will take care of itself and save you from racking up power bills.

Overheat Protection

Cosori air fryers are designed to guarantee maximum safety in your kitchen. Their fryers automatically shut down when they overheat to prevent outbreaks. You only need to let the air fryer cool down completely in such instances before using it again.

One-touch Cooking

Getting perfect air frying results depends on getting two important settings right: temperature and duration. With the Cosori air fryer, you can avoid the hassle of figuring out the right combination of settings. This Cosori air fryer product comes preprogrammed with several preset convenient cooking functions you can activate with a single touch. Professional chefs finely tune each of these functions and are guaranteed to give you the tastiest results. And if you want to make a personal choice recipe, you can set your preferred temperature and time, giving you the best of both worlds.

Different Models of Cosori Air Fryer

Cosori has several air fryers, making choosing one a little tricky. However, you can rest assured that these models have the same basic operation process. Choosing one that works perfectly for you would then depend on other non-basic variables like cooking capacity, the number of cooking preset programs preinstalled, price, and so on.

If, for instance, you have a large family and you'd like an air fryer that can make a meal for the whole family in one go, then the Cosori Dual Blaze 6.8-Quart Air Fryer might be ideal for you. In addition to its capacity, it is WiFi enabled and has the aesthetic brilliance that can upgrade the appearance of your kitchen.

If pricing is a big deal for you and you live alone, you may find the Cosori 3.7-Quart Air Fryer and the Cosori 3.4-Quart Air Fryer CO134-AF quite appealing. These products offer most of the distinct features of the Cosori brand in a compact size and at affordable prices. However, they don't come with the one-touch cooking functions that the dual blaze and other similar models offer.

If you're looking for the middle ground between the high-end dual blaze and the 3.4 Quart air fryer on the other end, you may consider the Cosori Premium 5.8-Quart Air Fryer or the Cosori Pro LE 5-Quart Air Fryer. The premium model offers you close to what the dual blaze offers. The differences are in the capacity, the number of recipe presets, and, of course, the price.

Cosori Air Fryer Cooking Tips

You can get the best results out of your Cosori air fryer and make the most amazing recipes with the following tips:

Preparation For First Use

If you're going to make the most effective use of your air fryer, you have to get things right from the setup stage. The following guidelines can help you at this stage.

♦ Find the perfect place for the air fryer. This is the first thing you should do after opening up your Cosori air fryer package. The air fryer requires a stable, level, heat-resistant surface away from walls and other furniture that may be damaged by steam. Also, ensure that the exhaust vent isn't close to any other object.

♦ Do a thorough clean-up. Once you've picked the perfect spot for your air fryer, cleaning the baskets is next. Start by pulling the handle to remove the baskets, then remove all plastic from the baskets before pressing the basket release button to separate both baskets. Use a dishwasher or a non-abrasive sponge to wash the baskets thoroughly. Then, use a slightly moist cloth to wipe the inside and outside of the air dryer before drying with a towel. When all this is done, return the baskets to the air fryer.

♦ Do a test run. Using the operating manual as a guide, do a test run of your appliance to ensure it works correctly and become familiar with its operation.

Preheating

A preheating process must precede all air frying to warm up the appliance. Exceptions can be made in cases where the appliance is already warm from previous use. After plugging it in, you can preheat your air fryer in two easy steps. Push the power button to turn the appliance on and press the preheat button. The default preheat setting will last 5 minutes, after which the appliance will beep thrice.

Air Frying

After preheating your air fryer, you're ready to start cooking. Take note of the following tips at this stage.

♦ Don't stuff the basket. The first step at this stage is to fill the basket with food. Take care not to stuff up the basket in a bid to get more items in at once. Doing so can lead to undesirable results, as it can prevent the heat from circulating properly.

♦ Avoid filling the basket with liquid. Your air fryer may be similar to your deep fryer, but both appliances work differently. So, you don't need to fill the baskets with oil or frying fat.

♦ Choose a setting. After pushing the baskets back into the air fryer, select a preset cooking program or customize the temperature and time. Press the Temp/Time button once to set the temperature and press it again to set the time.

Shaking

Shaking is an essential part of the air frying process, as it ensures that your food gets cooked evenly. When using a preset program, you'd get reminders to shake during cooking. If not, you'd have to decide on an appropriate time to shake the food. If the baskets are too heavy to shake, you can use tongs to mix or flip the food.

How to Care for and Clean Your Cosori Air Fryer

Taking proper care of your Cosori air fryer is the only way to guarantee you continue to get value for your money for as long as possible. Like most other air fryer brands, it's recommended that you clean the appliance, including the baskets and its interior, after every use to prevent permanent dents from dirt.

Before cleaning, ensure that the air fryer is completely cool. You can hasten the cooling process by pulling out the baskets after turning off the appliance. Clean the outside of the air fryer with a moist towel. The baskets can go into a dishwasher. Alternatively, wash them with hot, soapy water and a non-abrasive sponge.

For stubborn stains, you can make a spreadable paste of baking soda and water, which you can then spread over the baskets and leave to sit for 15 minutes before scrubbing and rinsing. Do not leave out the interior of the appliance in this cleaning process. A slightly moist towel would do just fine here. All this cleaning can leave some wetness in and around your air fryer, so ensure you do not use it immediately after cleaning. It's safer to let it dry before using it again.

Cosori Air Fryer Commonly Asked Questions & Answers

In this section, I provide answers to some frequently asked questions about Cosori air fryers to guide you.

Where is Cosori from?

Cosori is a kitchen appliances company that operates out of Southern California. The company launched its first air fryer in 2018 and quickly became a leading brand, winning the 2019 Red Dot Product Design Award and the 2019 Amazon Home Vendor Summit's "Best in Class New Item Launch. The brand has also won over many customers, evidenced by its impressive 4.7-star rating and over 1000 reviews on Amazon.

Can you put foil in a Cosori air fryer?

Yes, you can use foil to line the outer basket, as it can make cleaning up after use much easier. The convection process is conducive to using aluminum foil, provided it is secured to prevent it from loosening up and flying around in the device while cooking.

Are Cosori air fryers noisy?

Cosori air fryers are not noisy enough to constitute a nuisance. Several users have described the noise levels as 'barely noticeable,' and I did not find it a bother either. It's no louder than my electric oven. It rarely runs long enough during each use to become irritating anyway.

Do Cosori air fryers use Teflon?

Cosori air fryers are coated with BPA-free, non-stick Teflon. This coating makes cleaning the baskets quite easy. And if you're worried about the safety of the coating, you needn't be. The PFOA component of Teflon products that raise safety concerns has since been discontinued, making them all safe for domestic use.

Chapter 2 Breakfasts

Chapter 2 Breakfasts

Italian Egg Cups

Prep time: 5 minutes | Cook time: 10 minutes | Serves 4

Olive oil
235 ml marinara sauce
4 eggs
4 tablespoons shredded
Mozzarella cheese
4 teaspoons grated Parmesan cheese
Salt and freshly ground black pepper, to taste
Chopped fresh basil, for garnish

1. Lightly spray 4 individual ramekins with olive oil. 2. Pour 60 ml marinara sauce into each ramekin. 3. Crack one egg into each ramekin on top of the marinara sauce. 4. Sprinkle 1 tablespoon of Mozzarella and 1 tablespoon of Parmesan on top of each egg. Season with salt and pepper. 5. Cover each ramekin with aluminum foil. Place two of the ramekins in the air fryer basket. 6. Cook at 176°C for 5 minutes and remove the aluminum foil. Cook until the top is lightly browned and the egg white is cooked, another 2 to 4 minutes. If you prefer the yolk to be firmer, cook for 3 to 5 more minutes. 7. Repeat with the remaining two ramekins. Garnish with basil and serve.

Baked Potato Breakfast Boats

Prep time: 10 minutes | Cook time: 20 minutes | Serves 4

2 large white potatoes, scrubbed
Olive oil
Salt and freshly ground black pepper, to taste
4 eggs
2 tablespoons chopped, cooked bacon
235 ml shredded Cheddar cheese

1. Poke holes in the potatoes with a fork and microwave on full power for 5 minutes. 2. Turn potatoes over and cook an additional 3 to 5 minutes, or until the potatoes are fork-tender. 3. Cut the potatoes in half lengthwise and use a spoon to scoop out the inside of the potato. Be careful to leave a layer of potato so that it makes a sturdy "boat." 4. Preheat the air fryer to 176°C. 5. Lightly spray the air fryer basket with olive oil. Spray the skin side of the potatoes with oil and sprinkle with salt and pepper to taste. 6. Place the potato skins in the air fryer basket, skin-side down. Crack one egg into each potato skin. 7. Sprinkle ½ tablespoon of bacon pieces and 60 ml shredded cheese on top of each egg. Sprinkle with salt and pepper to taste. 8. Cook until the yolk is slightly runny, 5 to 6 minutes, or until the yolk is fully cooked, 7 to 10 minutes.

Homemade Toaster Pastries

Prep time: 10 minutes | Cook time: 11 minutes | Makes 6 pastries

Oil, for spraying
1 (425 g) package refrigerated piecrust
6 tablespoons jam or preserves of choice
475 ml icing sugar
3 tablespoons milk
1 to 2 tablespoons sprinkles of choice

1. Preheat the air fryer to 176°C. Line the air fryer basket with parchment and spray lightly with oil. 2. Cut the piecrust into 12 rectangles, about 3 by 4 inches each. You will need to reroll the dough scraps to get 12 rectangles. 3. Spread 1 tablespoon of jam in the center of 6 rectangles, leaving ¼ inch around the edges. 4. Pour some water into a small bowl. Use your finger to moisten the edge of each rectangle. 5. Top each rectangle with another and use your fingers to press around the edges. Using the tines of a fork, seal the edges of the dough and poke a few holes in the top of each one. Place the pastries in the prepared basket. 6. Cook for 11 minutes. Let cool completely. 7. In a medium bowl, whisk together the icing sugar and milk. Spread the icing over the tops of the pastries and add sprinkles. Serve immediately.

Quick and Easy Blueberry Muffins

Prep time: 10 minutes | Cook time: 12 minutes | Makes 8 muffins

315 ml flour
120 ml sugar
2 teaspoons baking powder
¼ teaspoon salt
80 ml rapeseed oil
1 egg
120 ml milk
160 ml blueberries, fresh or frozen and thawed

1. Preheat the air fryer to 166°C. 2. In a medium bowl, stir together flour, sugar, baking powder, and salt. 3. In a separate bowl, combine oil, egg, and milk and mix well. 4. Add egg mixture to dry ingredients and stir just until moistened. 5. Gently stir in the blueberries. 6. Spoon batter evenly into parchment paper-lined muffin cups. 7. Put 4 muffin cups in air fryer basket and cook for 12 minutes or until tops spring back when touched lightly. 8. Repeat previous step to cook remaining muffins. 9. Serve immediately.

Ham and Cheese Crescents

Prep time: 5 minutes | Cook time: 7 minutes | Makes 8 rolls

Oil, for spraying

1 (230 g) can ready-to-cook croissants

4 slices wafer-thin ham

8 cheese slices

2 tablespoons unsalted butter, melted

1. Line the air fryer basket with parchment and spray lightly with oil. 2. Separate the dough into 8 pieces. 3. Tear the ham slices in half and place 1 piece on each piece of dough. Top each with 1 slice of cheese. 4. Roll up each piece of dough, starting on the wider side. 5. Place the rolls in the prepared basket. Brush with the melted butter. 6. Cook at 160°C for 6 to 7 minutes, or until puffed and golden brown and the cheese is melted.

French Toast Sticks

Prep time: 10 minutes | Cook time: 9 minutes | Serves 4

Oil, for spraying

6 large eggs

315 ml milk

2 teaspoons vanilla extract

1 teaspoon ground cinnamon

8 slices bread, cut into thirds

Syrup of choice, for serving

1. Preheat the air fryer to 188°C. Line the air fryer basket with parchment and spray lightly with oil. 2. In a shallow bowl, whisk the eggs, milk, vanilla, and cinnamon. 3. Dunk one piece of bread in the egg mixture, making sure to coat both sides. Work quickly so the bread doesn't get soggy. Immediately transfer the bread to the prepared basket. 4. Repeat with the remaining bread, making sure the pieces don't touch each other. You may need to work in batches, depending on the size of your air fryer. 5. Cook for 5 minutes, flip, and cook for another 3 to 4 minutes, until browned and crispy. 6. Serve immediately with your favorite syrup.

Bacon-and-Eggs Avocado

Prep time: 5 minutes | Cook time: 17 minutes | Serves 1

1 large egg

1 avocado, halved, peeled, and pitted

2 slices bacon

Fresh parsley, for serving (optional)

Sea salt flakes, for garnish (optional)

1. Spray the air fryer basket with avocado oil. Preheat the air fryer to 160°C. Fill a small bowl with cool water. 2. Soft-boil the egg: Place the egg in the air fryer basket. Cook for 6 minutes for a soft yolk or 7 minutes for a cooked yolk. Transfer the egg to the bowl of cool water and let sit for 2 minutes. Peel and set aside. 3. Use a spoon to carve out extra space in the center of the avocado halves until the cavities are big enough to fit the soft-boiled egg. Place the soft-boiled egg in the center of one half of the avocado and replace the other half of the avocado on top, so the avocado appears whole on the outside. 4. Starting at one end of the avocado, wrap the bacon around the avocado to completely cover it. Use toothpicks to hold the bacon in place. 5. Place the bacon-wrapped avocado in the air fryer basket and cook for 5 minutes. Flip the avocado over and cook for another 5 minutes, or until the bacon is cooked to your liking. Serve on a bed of fresh parsley, if desired, and sprinkle with salt flakes, if desired. 6. Best served fresh. Store extras in an airtight container in the fridge for up to 4 days. Reheat in a preheated 160°C air fryer for 4 minutes, or until heated through.

Veggie Frittata

Prep time: 7 minutes | Cook time: 21 to 23 minutes | Serves 2

Avocado oil spray

60 ml diced red onion

60 ml diced red pepper

60 ml finely chopped broccoli

4 large eggs

85 g shredded sharp Cheddar cheese, divided

½ teaspoon dried thyme

Sea salt and freshly ground black pepper, to taste

1. Spray a pan well with oil. Put the onion, pepper, and broccoli in the pan, place the pan in the air fryer, and set to 176°C. Cook for 5 minutes. 2. While the vegetables cook, beat the eggs in a medium bowl. Stir in half of the cheese, and season with the thyme, salt, and pepper. 3. Add the eggs to the pan and top with the remaining cheese. Set the air fryer to 176°C. Cook for 16 to 18 minutes, until cooked through.

Spinach Omelet

Prep time: 5 minutes | Cook time: 12 minutes | Serves 2

4 large eggs

350 ml chopped fresh spinach leaves

2 tablespoons peeled and chopped brown onion

2 tablespoons salted butter, melted

120 ml shredded mild Cheddar cheese

¼ teaspoon salt

1. In an ungreased round nonstick baking dish, whisk eggs. Stir in spinach, onion, butter, Cheddar, and salt. 2. Place dish into air fryer basket. Adjust the temperature to 160°C and cook for 12 minutes. Omelet will be done when browned on the top and firm in the middle. 3. Slice in half and serve warm on two medium plates.

Sausage and Cheese Balls

Prep time: 10 minutes | Cook time: 12 minutes | Makes 16 balls

450 g pork sausage meat, removed from casings
120 ml shredded Cheddar cheese
30 g full-fat cream cheese, softened
1 large egg

1. Mix all ingredients in a large bowl. Form into sixteen (1-inch) balls. Place the balls into the air fryer basket. 2. Adjust the temperature to 204°C and cook for 12 minutes. 3. Shake the basket two or three times during cooking. Sausage balls will be browned on the outside and have an internal temperature of at least 64°C when completely cooked. 4. Serve warm.

Egg White Cups

Prep time: 10 minutes | Cook time: 15 minutes | Serves 4

475 ml 100% liquid egg whites
3 tablespoons salted butter, melted
¼ teaspoon salt
¼ teaspoon onion granules
½ medium plum tomato, cored and diced
120 ml chopped fresh spinach leaves

1. In a large bowl, whisk egg whites with butter, salt, and onion granules. Stir in tomato and spinach, then pour evenly into four ramekins greased with cooking spray. 2. Place ramekins into air fryer basket. Adjust the temperature to 150°C and cook for 15 minutes. Eggs will be fully cooked and firm in the center when done. Serve warm.

Vanilla Granola

Prep time: 5 minutes | Cook time: 40 minutes | Serves 4

235 ml rolled oats
3 tablespoons maple syrup
1 tablespoon sunflower oil
1 tablespoon coconut sugar
¼ teaspoon vanilla
¼ teaspoon cinnamon
¼ teaspoon sea salt

1. Preheat the air fryer to 120°C. 2. Mix together the oats, maple syrup, sunflower oil, coconut sugar, vanilla, cinnamon, and sea salt in a medium bowl and stir to combine. Transfer the mixture to a baking pan. 3. Place the pan in the air fryer basket and cook for 40 minutes, or until the granola is mostly dry and lightly browned. Stir the granola four times during cooking. 4. Let the granola stand for 5 to 10 minutes before serving.

Sausage Stuffed Peppers

Prep time: 15 minutes | Cook time: 15 minutes | Serves 4

230 g spicy pork sausage meat, removed from casings
4 large eggs
110 g full-fat cream cheese, softened
60 ml tinned diced tomatoes,
drained
4 green peppers
8 tablespoons shredded chilli cheese
120 ml full-fat sour cream

1. In a medium skillet over medium heat, crumble and brown the sausage meat until no pink remains. Remove sausage and drain the fat from the pan. Crack eggs into the pan, scramble, and cook until no longer runny. 2. Place cooked sausage in a large bowl and fold in cream cheese. Mix in diced tomatoes. Gently fold in eggs. 3. Cut a 4-inch to 5-inch slit in the top of each pepper, removing the seeds and white membrane with a small knife. Separate the filling into four servings and spoon carefully into each pepper. Top each with 2 tablespoons cheese. 4. Place each pepper into the air fryer basket. 5. Adjust the temperature to 176°C and set the timer for 15 minutes. 6. Peppers will be soft and cheese will be browned when ready. Serve immediately with sour cream on top.

Banana-Nut Muffins

Prep time: 5 minutes | Cook time: 15 minutes | Makes 10 muffins

Oil, for spraying
2 very ripe bananas
120 ml packed light brown sugar
80 ml rapeseed oil or vegetable oil
1 large egg
1 teaspoon vanilla extract
180 ml plain flour
1 teaspoon baking powder
1 teaspoon ground cinnamon
120 ml chopped walnuts

1. Preheat the air fryer to 160°C. Spray 10 silicone muffin cups lightly with oil. 2. In a medium bowl, mash the bananas. Add the brown sugar, rapeseed oil, egg, and vanilla and stir to combine. 3. Fold in the flour, baking powder, and cinnamon until just combined. 4. Add the walnuts and fold a few times to distribute throughout the batter. 5. Divide the batter equally among the prepared muffin cups and place them in the basket. You may need to work in batches, depending on the size of your air fryer. 6. Cook for 15 minutes, or until golden brown and a toothpick inserted into the center of a muffin comes out clean. The air fryer tends to brown muffins more than the oven, so don't be alarmed if they are darker than you're used to. They will still taste great. 7. Let cool on a wire rack before serving.

Bacon, Cheese, and Avocado Melt

Prep time: 5 minutes | Cook time: 3 to 5 minutes | Serves 2

1 avocado

4 slices cooked bacon, chopped

2 tablespoons salsa

1 tablespoon double cream

60 ml shredded Cheddar cheese

1. Preheat the air fryer to 204°C. 2. Slice the avocado in half lengthwise and remove the stone. To ensure the avocado halves do not roll in the basket, slice a thin piece of skin off the base. 3. In a small bowl, combine the bacon, salsa, and cream. Divide the mixture between the avocado halves and top with the cheese. 4. Place the avocado halves in the air fryer basket and cook for 3 to 5 minutes until the cheese has melted and begins to brown. Serve warm.

Bacon and Spinach Egg Muffins

Prep time: 7 minutes | Cook time: 12 to 14 minutes | Serves 6

6 large eggs

60 ml double (whipping) cream

½ teaspoon sea salt

¼ teaspoon freshly ground black pepper

¼ teaspoon cayenne pepper

(optional)

180 ml frozen chopped spinach, thawed and drained

4 strips cooked bacon, crumbled

60 g shredded Cheddar cheese

1. In a large bowl (with a spout if you have one), whisk together the eggs, double cream, salt, black pepper, and cayenne pepper (if using). 2. Divide the spinach and bacon among 6 silicone muffin cups. Place the muffin cups in your air fryer basket. 3. Divide the egg mixture among the muffin cups. Top with the cheese. 4. Set the air fryer to 150°C. Cook for 12 to 14 minutes, until the eggs are set and cooked through.

Savory Sweet Potato Hash

Prep time: 15 minutes | Cook time: 18 minutes | Serves 6

2 medium sweet potatoes, peeled and cut into 1-inch cubes

½ green pepper, diced

½ red onion, diced

110 g baby mushrooms, diced

2 tablespoons olive oil

1 garlic clove, minced

½ teaspoon salt

½ teaspoon black pepper

½ tablespoon chopped fresh rosemary

1. Preheat the air fryer to 192°C. 2. In a large bowl, toss all ingredients together until the vegetables are well coated and seasonings distributed. 3. Pour the vegetables into the air fryer basket, making sure they are in a single even layer. (If using a smaller air fryer, you may need to do this in two batches.) 4. Cook for 9 minutes, then toss or flip the vegetables. Cook for 9 minutes more. 5. Transfer to a serving bowl or individual plates and enjoy.

Not-So-English Muffins

Prep time: 5 minutes | Cook time: 10 minutes | Serves 4

2 strips turkey bacon, cut in half crosswise

2 whole-grain English muffins, split

235 ml fresh baby spinach, long stems removed

¼ ripe pear, peeled and thinly sliced

4 slices low-moisture Mozzarella or other melting cheese

1. Place bacon strips in air fryer basket and cook at 200°C for 2 minutes. Check and separate strips if necessary so they cook evenly. Cook for 3 to 4 more minutes, until crispy. Remove and drain on paper towels. 2. Place split muffin halves in air fryer basket and cook for 2 minutes, just until lightly browned. 3. Open air fryer and top each muffin with a quarter of the baby spinach, several pear slices, a strip of bacon, and a slice of cheese. 4. Cook at 182°C for 1 to 2 minutes, until cheese completely melts.

Spinach and Mushroom Mini Quiche

Prep time: 10 minutes | Cook time: 15 minutes | Serves 4

1 teaspoon olive oil, plus more for spraying

235 ml coarsely chopped mushrooms

235 ml fresh baby spinach, shredded

4 eggs, beaten

120 ml shredded Cheddar cheese

120 ml shredded Mozzarella cheese

¼ teaspoon salt

¼ teaspoon black pepper

1. Spray 4 silicone baking cups with olive oil and set aside. 2. In a medium sauté pan over medium heat, warm 1 teaspoon of olive oil. Add the mushrooms and sauté until soft, 3 to 4 minutes. 3. Add the spinach and cook until wilted, 1 to 2 minutes. Set aside. 4. In a medium bowl, whisk together the eggs, Cheddar cheese, Mozzarella cheese, salt, and pepper. 5. Gently fold the mushrooms and spinach into the egg mixture. 6. Pour ¼ of the mixture into each silicone baking cup. 7. Place the baking cups into the air fryer basket and cook at 176°C for 5 minutes. Stir the mixture in each ramekin slightly and cook until the egg has set, an additional 3 to 5 minutes.

Simple Scotch Eggs

Prep time: 5 minutes | Cook time: 25 minutes | Serves 4

4 large hard boiled eggs	8 slices thick-cut bacon
1 (340 g) package pork sausage meat	4 wooden toothpicks, soaked in water for at least 30 minutes

1. Slice the sausage meat into four parts and place each part into a large circle. 2. Put an egg into each circle and wrap it in the sausage. Put in the refrigerator for 1 hour. 3. Preheat the air fryer to 234°C. 4. Make a cross with two pieces of thick-cut bacon. Put a wrapped egg in the center, fold the bacon over top of the egg, and secure with a toothpick. 5. Cook in the preheated air fryer for 25 minutes. 6. Serve immediately.

Bourbon Vanilla French Toast

Prep time: 15 minutes | Cook time: 6 minutes | Serves 4

2 large eggs	2 tablespoons bourbon
2 tablespoons water	1 teaspoon vanilla extract
160 ml whole or semi-skimmed milk	8 (1-inch-thick) French bread slices
1 tablespoon butter, melted	Cooking spray

1. Preheat the air fryer to 160°C. Line the air fryer basket with parchment paper and spray it with cooking spray. 2. Beat the eggs with the water in a shallow bowl until combined. Add the milk, melted butter, bourbon, and vanilla and stir to mix well. 3. Dredge 4 slices of bread in the batter, turning to coat both sides evenly. Transfer the bread slices onto the parchment paper. 4. Cook for 6 minutes until nicely browned. Flip the slices halfway through the cooking time. 5. Remove from the basket to a plate and repeat with the remaining 4 slices of bread. 6. Serve warm.

Portobello Eggs Benedict

Prep time: 10 minutes | Cook time: 10 to 14 minutes | Serves 2

1 tablespoon olive oil	pepper, to taste
2 cloves garlic, minced	2 large eggs
¼ teaspoon dried thyme	2 tablespoons grated Pecorino Romano cheese
2 portobello mushrooms, stems removed and gills scraped out	1 tablespoon chopped fresh parsley, for garnish
2 plum tomatoes, halved lengthwise	1 teaspoon truffle oil (optional)
Salt and freshly ground black	

1. Preheat the air fryer to 204°C. 2. In a small bowl, combine the olive oil, garlic, and thyme. Brush the mixture over the mushrooms and tomatoes until thoroughly coated. Season to taste with salt and freshly ground black pepper. 3. Arrange the vegetables, cut side up, in the air fryer basket. Crack an egg into the center of each mushroom and sprinkle with cheese. Cook for 10 to 14 minutes until the vegetables are tender and the whites are firm. When cool enough to handle, coarsely chop the tomatoes and place on top of the eggs. Scatter parsley on top and drizzle with truffle oil, if desired, just before serving.

Breakfast Meatballs

Prep time: 10 minutes | Cook time: 15 minutes | Makes 18 meatballs

450 g pork sausage meat, removed from casings	120 ml shredded sharp Cheddar cheese
½ teaspoon salt	30 g cream cheese, softened
¼ teaspoon ground black pepper	1 large egg, whisked

1. Combine all ingredients in a large bowl. Form mixture into eighteen 1-inch meatballs. 2. Place meatballs into ungreased air fryer basket. Adjust the temperature to 204°C and cook for 15 minutes, shaking basket three times during cooking. Meatballs will be browned on the outside and have an internal temperature of at least 64°C when completely cooked. Serve warm.

Baked Peach Oatmeal

Prep time: 5 minutes | Cook time: 30 minutes | Serves 6

Olive oil cooking spray	120 ml non-fat plain Greek yoghurt
475 ml certified gluten-free rolled oats	1 teaspoon vanilla extract
475 ml unsweetened almond milk	½ teaspoon ground cinnamon
60 ml honey, plus more for drizzling (optional)	¼ teaspoon salt
	350 ml diced peaches, divided, plus more for serving (optional)

1. Preheat the air fryer to 192°C. Lightly coat the inside of a 6-inch cake pan with olive oil cooking spray. 2. In a large bowl, mix together the oats, almond milk, honey, yoghurt, vanilla, cinnamon, and salt until well combined. 3. Fold in 180 ml peaches and then pour the mixture into the prepared cake pan. 4. Sprinkle the remaining peaches across the top of the oatmeal mixture. Cook in the air fryer for 30 minutes. 5. Allow to set and cool for 5 minutes before serving with additional fresh fruit and honey for drizzling, if desired.

Oat and Chia Porridge

Prep time: 10 minutes | Cook time: 5 minutes | Serves 4

2 tablespoons peanut butter	1 L milk
4 tablespoons honey	475 ml oats
1 tablespoon butter, melted	235 ml chia seeds

1. Preheat the air fryer to 200°C. 2. Put the peanut butter, honey, butter, and milk in a bowl and stir to mix. Add the oats and chia seeds and stir. 3. Transfer the mixture to a bowl and cook in the air fryer for 5 minutes. Give another stir before serving.

Double-Dipped Mini Cinnamon Biscuits

Prep time: 15 minutes | Cook time: 13 minutes | Makes 8 biscuits

475 ml blanched almond flour	1 large egg
120 ml liquid or powdered sweetener	1 teaspoon vanilla extract
1 teaspoon baking powder	3 teaspoons ground cinnamon
½ teaspoon fine sea salt	Glaze:
60 ml plus 2 tablespoons (¾ stick) very cold unsalted butter	120 ml powdered sweetener
60 ml unsweetened, unflavoured almond milk	60 ml double cream or unsweetened, unflavoured almond milk

1. Preheat the air fryer to 176°C. Line a pie pan that fits into your air fryer with parchment paper. 2. In a medium-sized bowl, mix together the almond flour, sweetener (if powdered; do not add liquid sweetener), baking powder, and salt. Cut the butter into ½-inch squares, then use a hand mixer to work the butter into the dry ingredients. When you are done, the mixture should still have chunks of butter. 3. In a small bowl, whisk together the almond milk, egg, and vanilla extract (if using liquid sweetener, add it as well) until blended. Using a fork, stir the wet ingredients into the dry ingredients until large clumps form. Add the cinnamon and use your hands to swirl it into the dough. 4. Form the dough into sixteen 1-inch balls and place them on the prepared pan, spacing them about ½ inch apart. (If you're using a smaller air fryer, work in batches if necessary.) Cook in the air fryer until golden, 10 to 13 minutes. Remove from the air fryer and let cool on the pan for at least 5 minutes. 5. While the biscuits bake, make the glaze: Place the powdered sweetener in a small bowl and slowly stir in the heavy cream with a fork. 6. When the biscuits have cooled somewhat, dip the tops into the glaze, allow it to dry a bit, and then dip again for a thick glaze. 7. Serve warm or at room temperature. Store unglazed biscuits in an airtight container in the refrigerator for up to 3 days or in the freezer for up to a month. Reheat in a preheated 176°C air fryer for 5 minutes, or until warmed through, and dip in the glaze as instructed above.

Asparagus and Bell Pepper Strata

Prep time: 10 minutes | Cook time: 14 to 20 minutes | Serves 4

8 large asparagus spears, trimmed and cut into 2-inch pieces	into ½-inch cubes
	3 egg whites
80 ml shredded carrot	1 egg
120 ml chopped red pepper	3 tablespoons 1% milk
2 slices wholemeal bread, cut	½ teaspoon dried thyme

1. In a baking pan, combine the asparagus, carrot, red bell pepper, and 1 tablespoon of water. Cook in the air fryer at 166°C for 3 to 5 minutes, or until crisp-tender. Drain well. 2. Add the bread cubes to the vegetables and gently toss. 3. In a medium bowl, whisk the egg whites, egg, milk, and thyme until frothy. 4. Pour the egg mixture into the pan. Cook for 11 to 15 minutes, or until the strata is slightly puffy and set and the top starts to brown. Serve.

Sirloin Steaks with Eggs

Prep time: 8 minutes | Cook time: 14 minutes per batch | Serves 4

Cooking oil spray	1 teaspoon freshly ground black pepper, divided
4 (110 g) sirloin steaks	
1 teaspoon granulated garlic, divided	4 eggs
	½ teaspoon paprika
1 teaspoon salt, divided	

1. Insert the crisper plate into the basket and the basket into the unit. Preheat the unit by selecting AIR FRY, setting the temperature to 182°C, and setting the time to 3 minutes. Select START/STOP to begin. 2. Once the unit is preheated, spray the crisper plate with cooking oil. Place 2 steaks into the basket; do not oil or season them at this time. 3. Select AIR FRY, set the temperature to 182°C, and set the time to 9 minutes. Select START/STOP to begin. 4. After 5 minutes, open the unit and flip the steaks. Sprinkle each with ¼ teaspoon of granulated garlic, ¼ teaspoon of salt, and ¼ teaspoon of pepper. Resume cooking until the steaks register at least 64°C on a food thermometer. 5. When the cooking is complete, transfer the steaks to a plate and tent with aluminum foil to keep warm. Repeat steps 2, 3, and 4 with the remaining steaks. 6. Spray 4 ramekins with olive oil. Crack 1 egg into each ramekin. Sprinkle the eggs with the paprika and remaining ½ teaspoon each of salt and pepper. Working in batches, place 2 ramekins into the basket. 7. Select BAKE, set the temperature to 166°C, and set the time to 5 minutes. Select START/STOP to begin. 8. When the cooking is complete and the eggs are cooked to 72°C, remove the ramekins and repeat step 7 with the remaining 2 ramekins. 9. Serve the eggs with the steaks.

Broccoli-Mushroom Frittata

Prep time: 10 minutes | Cook time: 20 minutes | Serves 2

1 tablespoon olive oil
350 ml broccoli florets, finely chopped
120 ml sliced brown mushrooms
60 ml finely chopped onion

½ teaspoon salt
¼ teaspoon freshly ground black pepper
6 eggs
60 ml Parmesan cheese

1. In a nonstick cake pan, combine the olive oil, broccoli, mushrooms, onion, salt, and pepper. Stir until the vegetables are thoroughly coated with oil. Place the cake pan in the air fryer basket and set the air fryer to 204ºC. Cook for 5 minutes until the vegetables soften. 2. Meanwhile, in a medium bowl, whisk the eggs and Parmesan until thoroughly combined. Pour the egg mixture into the pan and shake gently to distribute the vegetables. Cook for another 15 minutes until the eggs are set. 3. Remove from the air fryer and let sit for 5 minutes to cool slightly. Use a silicone spatula to gently lift the frittata onto a plate before serving.

Gyro Breakfast Patties with Tzatziki

Prep time: 10 minutes | Cook time: 20 minutes per batch | Makes 16

patties
Patties:
900 g lamb or beef mince
120 ml diced red onions
60 ml sliced black olives
2 tablespoons tomato sauce
1 teaspoon dried oregano leaves
2 cloves garlic, minced
1 teaspoon fine sea salt
Tzatziki:

235 ml full-fat sour cream
1 small cucumber, chopped
½ teaspoon fine sea salt
½ teaspoon garlic powder, or 1 clove garlic, minced
¼ teaspoon dried dill, or 1 teaspoon finely chopped fresh dill
For Garnish/Serving:
120 ml crumbled feta cheese (about 60 g)
Diced red onions
Sliced black olives
Sliced cucumbers

1. Preheat the air fryer to 176ºC. 2. Place the lamb, onions, olives, tomato sauce, oregano, garlic, and salt in a large bowl. Mix well to combine the ingredients. 3. Using your hands, form the mixture into sixteen 3-inch patties. Place about 5 of the patties in the air fryer and cook for 20 minutes, flipping halfway through. Remove the patties and place them on a serving platter. Repeat with the remaining patties. 4. While the patties cook, make the tzatziki: Place all the ingredients in a small bowl and stir well. Cover and store in the fridge until ready to serve. Garnish with ground black pepper before serving. 5. Serve the patties with a dollop of tzatziki, a sprinkle of crumbled feta cheese, diced red onions, sliced black olives, and sliced cucumbers. 6. Store leftovers in an airtight container in the refrigerator for up to 5 days or in the freezer for up to a month. Reheat the patties in a preheated 200ºC air fryer for a few minutes, until warmed through.

Chapter 3 Vegetables and Sides

Chapter 3 Vegetables and Sides

Polenta Casserole

Prep time: 5 minutes | Cook time: 28 to 30 minutes | Serves 4

10 fresh asparagus spears, cut into 1-inch pieces
320 g cooked polenta, cooled to room temperature
1 egg, beaten
2 teaspoons Worcestershire
sauce
½ teaspoon garlic powder
¼ teaspoon salt
2 slices emmental cheese (about 40 g)
Oil for misting or cooking spray

1. Mist asparagus spears with oil and cook at 200ºC for 5 minutes, until crisp-tender. 2. In a medium bowl, mix together the grits, egg, Worcestershire, garlic powder, and salt. 3. Spoon half of polenta mixture into a baking pan and top with asparagus. 4. Tear cheese slices into pieces and layer evenly on top of asparagus. 5. Top with remaining polenta. 6. Cook at 180ºC for 23 to 25 minutes. The casserole will rise a little as it cooks. When done, the top will have browned lightly with just a hint of crispiness.

Blackened Courgette with Kimchi-Herb Sauce

Prep time: 10 minutes | Cook time: 15 minutes | Serves 2

2 medium courgettes, ends trimmed (about 170 g each)
2 tablespoons olive oil
75 g kimchi, finely chopped
5 g finely chopped fresh coriander
5 g finely chopped fresh flat-leaf
parsley, plus more for garnish
2 tablespoons rice vinegar
2 teaspoons Asian chili-garlic sauce
1 teaspoon grated fresh ginger
coarse sea salt and freshly ground black pepper, to taste

1. Brush the courgettes with half of the olive oil, place in the air fryer, and cook at 200ºC, turning halfway through, until lightly charred on the outside and tender, about 15 minutes. 2. Meanwhile, in a small bowl, combine the remaining 1 tablespoon olive oil, the kimchi, coriander, parsley, vinegar, chili-garlic sauce, and ginger. 3. Once the courgette is finished cooking, transfer it to a colander and let it cool for 5 minutes. Using your fingers, pinch and break the courgette into bite-size pieces, letting them fall back into the colander. Season the courgette with salt and pepper, toss to combine, then let sit a further 5 minutes to allow some of its liquid to drain. Pile the courgette atop the kimchi sauce on a plate and sprinkle with more parsley to serve.

Buttery Green Beans

Prep time: 5 minutes | Cook time: 8 to 10 minutes | Serves 6

450 g green beans, trimmed
1 tablespoon avocado oil
1 teaspoon garlic powder
Sea salt and freshly ground black pepper, to taste
4 tablespoons unsalted butter, melted
20 g freshly grated Parmesan cheese

1. In a large bowl, toss together the green beans, avocado oil, and garlic powder and season with salt and pepper. 2. Set the air fryer to 200ºC. Arrange the green beans in a single layer in the air fryer basket. Cook for 8 to 10 minutes, tossing halfway through. 3. Transfer the beans to a large bowl and toss with the melted butter. Top with the Parmesan cheese and serve warm.

Turnip Fries

Prep time: 10 minutes | Cook time: 20 to 30 minutes | Serves 4

900 g turnip, peeled and cut into ¼ to ½-inch fries
2 tablespoons olive oil
Salt and freshly ground black pepper, to taste

1. Preheat the air fryer to 200ºC. 2. In a large bowl, combine the turnip and olive oil. Season to taste with salt and black pepper. Toss gently until thoroughly coated. 3. Working in batches if necessary, spread the turnip in a single layer in the air fryer basket. Pausing halfway through the cooking time to shake the basket, cook for 20 to 30 minutes until the fries are lightly browned and crunchy.

Roasted Aubergine

Prep time: 15 minutes | Cook time: 15 minutes | Serves 4

1 large aubergine
2 tablespoons olive oil
¼ teaspoon salt
½ teaspoon garlic powder

1. Remove top and bottom from aubergine. Slice aubergine into ¼-inch-thick round slices. 2. Brush slices with olive oil. Sprinkle with salt and garlic powder. Place aubergine slices into the air fryer basket. 3. Adjust the temperature to 200ºCand set the timer for 15 minutes. 4. Serve immediately.

Crispy Lemon Artichoke Hearts

Prep time: 10 minutes | Cook time: 15 minutes | Serves 2

1 (425 g) can artichoke hearts in water, drained
1 egg
1 tablespoon water
30 g whole wheat bread crumbs
¼ teaspoon salt
¼ teaspoon paprika
½ lemon

1. Preheat the air fryer to 192ºC. 2. In a medium shallow bowl, beat together the egg and water until frothy. 3. In a separate medium shallow bowl, mix together the bread crumbs, salt, and paprika. 4. Dip each artichoke heart into the egg mixture, then into the bread crumb mixture, coating the outside with the crumbs. Place the artichokes hearts in a single layer of the air fryer basket. 5. Fry the artichoke hearts for 15 minutes. 6. Remove the artichokes from the air fryer, and squeeze fresh lemon juice over the top before serving.

Roasted Potatoes and Asparagus

Prep time: 5 minutes | Cook time: 23 minutes | Serves 4

4 medium potatoes
1 bunch asparagus
75 g cottage cheese
80 g low-fat crème fraiche
1 tablespoon wholegrain mustard
Salt and pepper, to taste
Cooking spray

1. Preheat the air fryer to 200ºC. Spritz the air fryer basket with cooking spray. 2. Place the potatoes in the basket. Cook the potatoes for 20 minutes. 3. Boil the asparagus in salted water for 3 minutes. 4. Remove the potatoes and mash them with rest of ingredients. Sprinkle with salt and pepper. 5. Serve immediately.

Five-Spice Roasted Sweet Potatoes

Prep time: 10 minutes | Cook time: 12 minutes | Serves 4

½ teaspoon ground cinnamon
¼ teaspoon ground cumin
¼ teaspoon paprika
1 teaspoon chili powder
⅛ teaspoon turmeric
½ teaspoon salt (optional)
Freshly ground black pepper, to taste
2 large sweet potatoes, peeled and cut into ¾-inch cubes
1 tablespoon olive oil

1. In a large bowl, mix together cinnamon, cumin, paprika, chili powder, turmeric, salt, and pepper to taste. 2. Add potatoes and stir well. 3. Drizzle the seasoned potatoes with the olive oil and stir until evenly coated. 4. Place seasoned potatoes in a baking pan or an ovenproof dish that fits inside your air fryer basket. 5. Cook for 6 minutes at 200ºC, stop, and stir well. 6. Cook for an additional 6 minutes.

Potato with Creamy Cheese

Prep time: 5 minutes | Cook time: 15 minutes | Serves 2

2 medium potatoes
1 teaspoon butter
3 tablespoons sour cream
1 teaspoon chives
1½ tablespoons grated Parmesan cheese

1. Preheat the air fryer to 180ºC. 2. Pierce the potatoes with a fork and boil them in water until they are cooked. 3. Transfer to the air fryer and cook for 15 minutes. 4. In the meantime, combine the sour cream, cheese and chives in a bowl. Cut the potatoes halfway to open them up and fill with the butter and sour cream mixture. 5. Serve immediately.

Parmesan and Herb Sweet Potatoes

Prep time: 10 minutes | Cook time: 18 minutes | Serves 4

2 large sweet potatoes, peeled and cubed
65 ml olive oil
1 teaspoon dried rosemary
½ teaspoon salt
2 tablespoons shredded Parmesan

1. Preheat the air fryer to 180ºC. 2. In a large bowl, toss the sweet potatoes with the olive oil, rosemary, and salt. 3. Pour the potatoes into the air fryer basket and cook for 10 minutes, then stir the potatoes and sprinkle the Parmesan over the top. Continue roasting for 8 minutes more. 4. Serve hot and enjoy.

Tofu Bites

Prep time: 15 minutes | Cook time: 30 minutes | Serves 4

1 packaged firm tofu, cubed and pressed to remove excess water
1 tablespoon soy sauce
1 tablespoon ketchup
1 tablespoon maple syrup
½ teaspoon vinegar
1 teaspoon liquid smoke
1 teaspoon hot sauce
2 tablespoons sesame seeds
1 teaspoon garlic powder
Salt and ground black pepper, to taste
Cooking spray

1. Preheat the air fryer to 192ºC. 2. Spritz a baking dish with cooking spray. 3. Combine all the ingredients to coat the tofu completely and allow the marinade to absorb for half an hour. 4. Transfer the tofu to the baking dish, then cook for 15 minutes. Flip the tofu over and cook for another 15 minutes on the other side. 5. Serve immediately.

Cheesy Loaded Broccoli

Prep time: 10 minutes | Cook time: 10 minutes | Serves 2

215 g fresh broccoli florets
1 tablespoon coconut oil
¼ teaspoon salt
120 g shredded sharp Cheddar cheese

60 g sour cream
4 slices cooked sugar-free bacon, crumbled
1 medium spring onion, trimmed and sliced on the bias

1. Place broccoli into ungreased air fryer basket, drizzle with coconut oil, and sprinkle with salt. Adjust the temperature to 180ºC and cook for 8 minutes. Shake basket three times during cooking to avoid burned spots. 2. Sprinkle broccoli with Cheddar and cook for 2 additional minutes. When done, cheese will be melted and broccoli will be tender. 3. Serve warm in a large serving dish, topped with sour cream, crumbled bacon, and spring onion slices.

Southwestern Roasted Corn

Prep time: 10 minutes | Cook time: 10 minutes | Serves 4

Corn:
240 g thawed frozen corn kernels
50 g diced yellow onion
150 g mixed diced bell peppers
1 jalapeño, diced
1 tablespoon fresh lemon juice
1 teaspoon ground cumin

½ teaspoon ancho chili powder
½ teaspoon coarse sea salt
For Serving:
150 g queso fresco or feta cheese
10 g chopped fresh coriander
1 tablespoon fresh lemon juice

1. For the corn: In a large bowl, stir together the corn, onion, bell peppers, jalapeño, lemon juice, cumin, chili powder, and salt until well incorporated. 2. Pour the spiced vegetables into the air fryer basket. Set the air fryer to 192ºC for 10 minutes, stirring halfway through the cooking time. 3. Transfer the corn mixture to a serving bowl. Add the cheese, coriander, and lemon juice and stir well to combine. Serve immediately.

Parsnip Fries with Romesco Sauce

Prep time: 20 minutes | Cook time: 24 minutes | Serves 4

Romesco Sauce:
1 red pepper, halved and seeded
1 (1-inch) thick slice of Italian bread, torn into pieces
130 g almonds, toasted
Olive oil
½ Jalapeño pepper, seeded

1 tablespoon fresh parsley leaves
1 clove garlic
2 plum tomatoes, peeled and seeded
1 tablespoon red wine vinegar
¼ teaspoon smoked paprika

½ teaspoon salt
180 ml olive oil
3 parsnips, peeled and cut into long strips

2 teaspoons olive oil
Salt and freshly ground black pepper, to taste

1. Preheat the air fryer to 200ºC. 2. Place the red pepper halves, cut side down, in the air fryer basket and cook for 8 to 10 minutes, or until the skin turns black all over. Remove the pepper from the air fryer and let it cool. When it is cool enough to handle, peel the pepper. 3. Toss the torn bread and almonds with a little olive oil and cook for 4 minutes, shaking the basket a couple times throughout the cooking time. When the bread and almonds are nicely toasted, remove them from the air fryer and let them cool for just a minute or two. 4. Combine the toasted bread, almonds, roasted red pepper, Jalapeño pepper, parsley, garlic, tomatoes, vinegar, smoked paprika and salt in a food processor or blender. Process until smooth. With the processor running, add the olive oil through the feed tube until the sauce comes together in a smooth paste that is barely pourable. 5. Toss the parsnip strips with the olive oil, salt and freshly ground black pepper and cook at 200ºC for 10 minutes, shaking the basket a couple times during the cooking process so they brown and cook evenly. Serve the parsnip fries warm with the Romesco sauce to dip into.

Shishito Pepper Roast

Prep time: 4 minutes | Cook time: 9 minutes | Serves 4

Cooking oil spray (sunflower, safflower, or refined coconut)
450 g shishito, Anaheim, or bell peppers, rinsed

1 tablespoon soy sauce
2 teaspoons freshly squeezed lime juice
2 large garlic cloves, pressed

1. Insert the crisper plate into the basket and the basket into the unit. Preheat the unit by selecting AIR ROAST, setting the temperature to 200ºC, and setting the time to 3 minutes. Select START/STOP to begin. 2. Once the unit is preheated, spray the crisper plate and the basket with cooking oil. Place the peppers into the basket and spray them with oil. 3. Select AIR ROAST, set the temperature to 200ºC, and set the time to 9 minutes. Select START/STOP to begin. 4. After 3 minutes, remove the basket and shake the peppers. Spray the peppers with more oil. Reinsert the basket to resume cooking. Repeat this step again after 3 minutes. 5. While the peppers roast, in a medium bowl, whisk the soy sauce, lime juice, and garlic until combined. Set aside. 6. When the cooking is complete, several of the peppers should have lots of nice browned spots on them. If using Anaheim or bell peppers, cut a slit in the side of each pepper and remove the seeds, which can be bitter. 7. Place the roasted peppers in the bowl with the sauce. Toss to coat the peppers evenly and serve.

Spiced Honey-Walnut Carrots

Prep time: 5 minutes | Cook time: 12 minutes | Serves 6

450 g baby carrots
2 tablespoons olive oil
80 g raw honey

¼ teaspoon ground cinnamon
25 g black walnuts, chopped

1. Preheat the air fryer to 180ºC. 2. In a large bowl, toss the baby carrots with olive oil, honey, and cinnamon until well coated. 3. Pour into the air fryer and cook for 6 minutes. Shake the basket, sprinkle the walnuts on top, and cook for 6 minutes more. 4. Remove the carrots from the air fryer and serve.

Rosemary-Roasted Red Potatoes

Prep time: 5 minutes | Cook time: 20 minutes | Serves 6

450 g red potatoes, quartered
65 ml olive oil
½ teaspoon coarse sea salt

¼ teaspoon black pepper
1 garlic clove, minced
4 rosemary sprigs

1. Preheat the air fryer to 180ºC. 2. In a large bowl, toss the potatoes with the olive oil, salt, pepper, and garlic until well coated. 3. Pour the potatoes into the air fryer basket and top with the sprigs of rosemary. 4. Cook for 10 minutes, then stir or toss the potatoes and cook for 10 minutes more. 5. Remove the rosemary sprigs and serve the potatoes. Season with additional salt and pepper, if needed.

Golden Pickles

Prep time: 10 minutes | Cook time: 15 minutes | Serves 4

14 dill pickles, sliced
30 g flour
⅛ teaspoon baking powder
Pinch of salt
2 tablespoons cornflour plus 3

tablespoons water
6 tablespoons panko bread crumbs
½ teaspoon paprika
Cooking spray

1. Preheat the air fryer to 200ºC. 2. Drain any excess moisture out of the dill pickles on a paper towel. 3. In a bowl, combine the flour, baking powder and salt. 4. Throw in the cornflour and water mixture and combine well with a whisk. 5. Put the panko bread crumbs in a shallow dish along with the paprika. Mix thoroughly. 6. Dip the pickles in the flour batter, before coating in the bread crumbs. Spritz all the pickles with the cooking spray. 7. Transfer to the air fryer basket and cook for 15 minutes, or until golden brown. 8. Serve immediately.

pinach and Cheese Stuffed Tomatoes

Prep time: 20 minutes | Cook time: 15 minutes | Serves 2

4 ripe beefsteak tomatoes
¾ teaspoon black pepper
½ teaspoon coarse sea salt
1 (280 g) package frozen chopped spinach, thawed and squeezed dry

1 (150 g) package garlic-and-herb Boursin cheese
3 tablespoons sour cream
45 g finely grated Parmesan cheese

1. Cut the tops off the tomatoes. Using a small spoon, carefully remove and discard the pulp. Season the insides with ½ teaspoon of the black pepper and ¼ teaspoon of the salt. Invert the tomatoes onto paper towels and allow to drain while you make the filling. 2. Meanwhile, in a medium bowl, combine the spinach, Boursin cheese, sour cream, ½ of the Parmesan, and the remaining ¼ teaspoon salt and ¼ teaspoon pepper. Stir until ingredients are well combined. Divide the filling among the tomatoes. Top with the remaining ½ of the Parmesan. 3. Place the tomatoes in the air fryer basket. Set the air fryer to 180ºC for 15 minutes, or until the filling is hot.

Breaded Green Tomatoes

Prep time: 15 minutes | Cook time: 30 minutes | Serves 4

60 g plain flour
2 eggs
60 g semolina
60 g panko bread crumbs
1 teaspoon garlic powder

Salt and freshly ground black pepper, to taste
2 green tomatoes, cut into ½-inch-thick rounds
Cooking oil spray

1. Place the flour in a small bowl. 2. In another small bowl, beat the eggs. 3. In a third small bowl, stir together the semolina, panko, and garlic powder. Season with salt and pepper. 4. Dip each tomato slice into the flour, the egg, and finally the semolina mixture to coat. 5. Insert the crisper plate into the basket and the basket into the unit. Preheat the unit by selecting AIR FRY, setting the temperature to 200ºC, and setting the time to 3 minutes. Select START/STOP to begin. 6. Once the unit is preheated, spray the crisper plate and the basket with cooking oil. Working in batches, place the tomato slices in the air fryer in a single layer. Do not stack them. Spray the tomato slices with the cooking oil. 7. Select AIR FRY, set the temperature to 200ºC, and set the time to 10 minutes. Select START/STOP to begin. 8. After 5 minutes, use tongs to flip the tomatoes. Resume cooking for 4 to 5 minutes, or until crisp. 9. When the cooking is complete, transfer the fried green tomatoes to a plate. Repeat steps 6, 7, and 8 for the remaining tomatoes.

Broccoli with Sesame Dressing

Prep time: 5 minutes | Cook time: 10 minutes | Serves 4

425 g broccoli florets, cut into bite-size pieces
1 tablespoon olive oil
¼ teaspoon salt
2 tablespoons sesame seeds
2 tablespoons rice vinegar

2 tablespoons coconut aminos
2 tablespoons sesame oil
½ teaspoon xylitol
¼ teaspoon red pepper flakes (optional)

1. Preheat the air fryer to 200°C. 2. In a large bowl, toss the broccoli with the olive oil and salt until thoroughly coated. 3. Transfer the broccoli to the air fryer basket. Pausing halfway through the cooking time to shake the basket, cook for 10 minutes until the stems are tender and the edges are beginning to crisp. 4. Meanwhile, in the same large bowl, whisk together the sesame seeds, vinegar, coconut aminos, sesame oil, xylitol, and red pepper flakes (if using). 5. Transfer the broccoli to the bowl and toss until thoroughly coated with the seasonings. Serve warm or at room temperature.

Zesty Fried Asparagus

Prep time: 3 minutes | Cook time: 10 minutes | Serves 4

Oil, for spraying
10 to 12 spears asparagus, trimmed
2 tablespoons olive oil

1 tablespoon garlic powder
1 teaspoon chili powder
½ teaspoon ground cumin
¼ teaspoon salt

1. Line the air fryer basket with parchment and spray lightly with oil. 2. If the asparagus are too long to fit easily in the air fryer, cut them in half. 3. Place the asparagus, olive oil, garlic, chili powder, cumin, and salt in a zip-top plastic bag, seal, and toss until evenly coated. 4. Place the asparagus in the prepared basket. 5. Cook at 200°C for 5 minutes, flip, and cook for another 5 minutes, or until bright green and firm but tender.

Crispy Garlic Sliced Aubergine

Prep time: 5 minutes | Cook time: 25 minutes | Serves 4

1 egg
1 tablespoon water
60 g whole wheat bread crumbs
1 teaspoon garlic powder
½ teaspoon dried oregano

½ teaspoon salt
½ teaspoon paprika
1 medium aubergine, sliced into ¼-inch-thick rounds
1 tablespoon olive oil

1. Preheat the air fryer to 180°C. 2. In a medium shallow bowl, beat together the egg and water until frothy. 3. In a separate medium shallow bowl, mix together bread crumbs, garlic powder, oregano, salt, and paprika. 4. Dip each aubergine slice into the egg mixture, then into the bread crumb mixture, coating the outside with crumbs. Place the slices in a single layer in the bottom of the air fryer basket. 5. Drizzle the tops of the aubergine slices with the olive oil, then fry for 15 minutes. Turn each slice and cook for an additional 10 minutes.

Dijon Roast Cabbage

Prep time: 10 minutes | Cook time: 10 minutes | Serves 4

1 small head cabbage, cored and sliced into 1-inch-thick slices
2 tablespoons olive oil, divided
½ teaspoon salt

1 tablespoon Dijon mustard
1 teaspoon apple cider vinegar
1 teaspoon granular erythritol

1. Drizzle each cabbage slice with 1 tablespoon olive oil, then sprinkle with salt. Place slices into ungreased air fryer basket, working in batches if needed. Adjust the temperature to 180°C and cook for 10 minutes. Cabbage will be tender and edges will begin to brown when done. 2. In a small bowl, whisk remaining olive oil with mustard, vinegar, and erythritol. Drizzle over cabbage in a large serving dish. Serve warm.

SAsian-Inspired Roasted Broccoli

Prep time: 10 minutes | Cook time: 15 minutes | Serves 4

Broccoli:
Oil, for spraying
450 g broccoli florets
2 teaspoons peanut oil
1 tablespoon minced garlic
½ teaspoon salt

Sauce:
2 tablespoons soy sauce
2 teaspoons honey
2 teaspoons Sriracha
1 teaspoon rice vinegar

Make the Broccoli 1. Line the air fryer basket with parchment and spray lightly with oil. 2. In a large bowl, toss together the broccoli, peanut oil, garlic, and salt until evenly coated. 3. Spread out the broccoli in an even layer in the prepared basket. 4. Cook at 200°C for 15 minutes, stirring halfway through. Make the Sauce 5. Meanwhile, in a small microwave-safe bowl, combine the soy sauce, honey, Sriracha, and rice vinegar and microwave on high for about 15 seconds. Stir to combine. 6. Transfer the broccoli to a serving bowl and add the sauce. Gently toss until evenly coated and serve immediately.

Gold Artichoke Hearts

Prep time: 15 minutes | Cook time: 8 minutes | Serves 4

12 whole artichoke hearts packed in water, drained
60 g plain flour
1 egg

40 g panko bread crumbs
1 teaspoon Italian seasoning
Cooking oil spray

1. Squeeze any excess water from the artichoke hearts and place them on paper towels to dry. 2. Place the flour in a small bowl. 3. In another small bowl, beat the egg. 4. In a third small bowl, stir together the panko and Italian seasoning. 5. Dip the artichoke hearts in the flour, in the egg, and into the panko mixture until coated. 6. Insert the crisper plate into the basket and the basket into the unit. Preheat the unit by selecting AIR FRY, setting the temperature to 192°C, and setting the time to 3 minutes. Select START/STOP to begin. 7. Once the unit is preheated, spray the crisper plate and the basket with cooking oil. Place the breaded artichoke hearts into the basket, stacking them if needed. 8. Select AIR FRY, set the temperature to 192°C, and set the time to 8 minutes. Select START/STOP to begin. 9. After 4 minutes, use tongs to flip the artichoke hearts. I recommend flipping instead of shaking because the hearts are small, and this will help keep the breading intact. Re-insert the basket to resume cooking. 10. When the cooking is complete, the artichoke hearts should be deep golden brown and crisp. Cool for 5 minutes before serving.

Spiced Butternut Squash

Prep time: 10 minutes | Cook time: 15 minutes | Serves 4

600 g 1-inch-cubed butternut squash
2 tablespoons vegetable oil

1 to 2 tablespoons brown sugar
1 teaspoon Chinese five-spice powder

1. In a medium bowl, combine the squash, oil, sugar, and five-spice powder. Toss to coat. 2. Place the squash in the air fryer basket. Set the air fryer to 200°C for 15 minutes or until tender.

Mashed Sweet Potato Tots

Prep time: 10 minutes | Cook time: 12 to 13 minutes per batch | Makes 18 to 24 tots

210 g cooked mashed sweet potatoes
1 egg white, beaten
⅛ teaspoon ground cinnamon
1 dash nutmeg

2 tablespoons chopped pecans
1½ teaspoons honey
Salt, to taste
50 g panko bread crumbs
Oil for misting or cooking spray

1. Preheat the air fryer to 200°C. 2. In a large bowl, mix together the potatoes, egg white, cinnamon, nutmeg, pecans, honey, and salt to taste. 3. Place panko crumbs on a sheet of wax paper. 4. For each tot, use about 2 teaspoons of sweet potato mixture. To shape, drop the measure of potato mixture onto panko crumbs and push crumbs up and around potatoes to coat edges. Then turn tot over to coat other side with crumbs. 5. Mist tots with oil or cooking spray and place in air fryer basket in single layer. 6. Cook at 200°C for 12 to 13 minutes, until browned and crispy. 7. Repeat steps 5 and 6 to cook remaining tots.

Stuffed Red Peppers with Herbed Ricotta and Tomatoes

Prep time: 10 minutes | Cook time: 20 minutes | Serves 4

2 red peppers
250 g cooked brown rice
2 plum tomatoes, diced
1 garlic clove, minced
¼ teaspoon salt
¼ teaspoon black pepper
115 g ricotta

3 tablespoons fresh basil, chopped
3 tablespoons fresh oregano, chopped
20 g shredded Parmesan, for topping

1. Preheat the air fryer to 180°C. 2. Cut the bell peppers in half and remove the seeds and stem. 3. In a medium bowl, combine the brown rice, tomatoes, garlic, salt, and pepper. 4. Distribute the rice filling evenly among the four bell pepper halves. 5. In a small bowl, combine the ricotta, basil, and oregano. Put the herbed cheese over the top of the rice mixture in each bell pepper. 6. Place the bell peppers into the air fryer and cook for 20 minutes. 7. Remove and serve with shredded Parmesan on top.

Asparagus Fries

Prep time: 15 minutes | Cook time: 5 to 7 minutes per batch | Serves 4

340 g fresh asparagus spears with tough ends trimmed off
2 egg whites
60 ml water
80 g panko bread crumbs

25 g grated Parmesan cheese, plus 2 tablespoons
¼ teaspoon salt
Oil for misting or cooking spray

1. Preheat the air fryer to 200°C. 2. In a shallow dish, beat egg whites and water until slightly foamy. 3. In another shallow dish, combine panko, Parmesan, and salt. 4. Dip asparagus spears in egg, then roll in crumbs. Spray with oil or cooking spray. 5. Place a layer of asparagus in air fryer basket, leaving just a little space in between each spear. Stack another layer on top, crosswise. Cook at 200°C for 5 to 7 minutes, until crispy and golden brown. 6. Repeat to cook remaining asparagus.

Chapter 4 Beef, Pork, and Lamb

Chapter 4 Beef, Pork, and Lamb

Macadamia Nuts Crusted Pork Rack

Prep time: 5 minutes | Cook time: 35 minutes | Serves 2

1 clove garlic, minced
2 tablespoons olive oil
450 g rack of pork
235 ml chopped macadamia nuts

1 tablespoon breadcrumbs
1 tablespoon rosemary, chopped
1 egg
Salt and ground black pepper, to taste

1. Preheat the air fryer to 176°C. 2. Combine the garlic and olive oil in a small bowl. Stir to mix well. 3. On a clean work surface, rub the pork rack with the garlic oil and sprinkle with salt and black pepper on both sides. 4. Combine the macadamia nuts, breadcrumbs, and rosemary in a shallow dish. Whisk the egg in a large bowl. 5. Dredge the pork in the egg, then roll the pork over the macadamia nut mixture to coat well. Shake the excess off. 6. Arrange the pork in the preheated air fryer and cook for 30 minutes on both sides. Increase to 200°C and fry for 5 more minutes or until the pork is well browned. 7. Serve immediately.

Steak Gyro Platter

Prep time: 30 minutes | Cook time: 8 to 10 minutes | Serves 4

450 g bavette or skirt steak
1 teaspoon garlic powder
1 teaspoon ground cumin
½ teaspoon sea salt
½ teaspoon freshly ground black pepper
140 g shredded romaine lettuce
120 ml crumbled feta cheese

120 ml peeled and diced cucumber
80 ml sliced red onion
60 ml seeded and diced tomato
2 tablespoons pitted and sliced black olives
Tzatziki sauce, for serving

1. Pat the steak dry with paper towels. In a small bowl, combine the garlic powder, cumin, salt, and pepper. Sprinkle this mixture all over the steak, and allow the steak to rest at room temperature for 45 minutes. 2. Preheat the air fryer to 204°C. Place the steak in the air fryer basket and cook for 4 minutes. Flip the steak and cook 4 to 6 minutes more, until an instant-read thermometer reads 49°C at the thickest point for medium-rare (or as desired). Remove the steak from the air fryer and let it rest for 5 minutes. 3. Divide the romaine among plates. Top with the feta, cucumber, red onion, tomato, and olives.

Kale and Beef Omelet

Prep time: 15 minutes | Cook time: 16 minutes | Serves 4

230 g leftover beef, coarsely chopped
2 garlic cloves, pressed
235 ml kale, torn into pieces and wilted
1 tomato, chopped
¼ teaspoon sugar

4 eggs, beaten
4 tablespoons double cream
½ teaspoon turmeric powder
Salt and ground black pepper, to taste
⅛ teaspoon ground allspice
Cooking spray

1. Preheat the air fryer to 182°C. Spritz four ramekins with cooking spray. 2. Put equal amounts of each of the ingredients into each ramekin and mix well. 3. Cook for 16 minutes. Serve immediately.

Sichuan Cumin Lamb

Prep time: 30 minutes | Cook time: 10 minutes | Serves 4

Lamb:
2 tablespoons cumin seeds
1 teaspoon Sichuan peppercorns, or ½ teaspoon cayenne pepper
450 g lamb (preferably shoulder), cut into ½ by 2-inch pieces
2 tablespoons vegetable oil
1 tablespoon light soy sauce

1 tablespoon minced garlic
2 fresh red chiles, chopped
1 teaspoon coarse or flaky salt
¼ teaspoon sugar
For Serving:
2 spring onionspring onions, chopped
Large handful of chopped fresh coriander

1. For the lamb: In a dry skillet, toast the cumin seeds and Sichuan peppercorns (if using) over medium heat, stirring frequently, until fragrant, 1 to 2 minutes. Remove from the heat and let cool. Use a mortar and pestle to coarsely grind the toasted spices. 2. Use a fork to pierce the lamb pieces to allow the marinade to penetrate better. In a large bowl or resealable plastic bag, combine the toasted spices, vegetable oil, soy sauce, garlic, chiles, salt, and sugar. Add the lamb to the bag. Seal and massage to coat. Marinate at room temperature for 30 minutes. 3. Place the lamb in a single layer in the air fryer basket. Set the air fryer to 176°C for 10 minutes. Use a meat thermometer to ensure the lamb has reached an internal temperature of 64°C (medium-rare). 4. Transfer the lamb to a serving bowl. Stir in the spring onionspring onions and coriander and serve.

Pork Loin with Aloha Salsa

Prep time: 20 minutes | Cook time: 7 to 9 minutes | Serves 4

Aloha Salsa:	2 eggs
235 ml fresh pineapple, chopped in small pieces	2 tablespoons milk
	60 ml flour
60 ml red onion, finely chopped	60 ml panko bread crumbs
60 ml green or red pepper, chopped	4 teaspoons sesame seeds
	450 g boneless, thin pork loin or
½ teaspoon ground cinnamon	tenderloin (⅜- to ½-inch thick)
1 teaspoon reduced-salt soy sauce	Pepper and salt
	60 ml cornflour
⅛ teaspoon crushed red pepper	Oil for misting or cooking spray
⅛ teaspoon ground black pepper	

1. In a medium bowl, stir together all ingredients for salsa. Cover and refrigerate while cooking pork. 2. Preheat the air fryer to 200ºC. 3. Beat together eggs and milk in shallow dish. 4. In another shallow dish, mix together the flour, panko, and sesame seeds. 5. Sprinkle pork with pepper and salt to taste. 6. Dip pork in cornflour, egg mixture, and then panko coating. Spray both sides with oil or cooking spray. 7. Cook pork for 3 minutes. Turn pork over, spraying both sides, and continue cooking for 4 to 6 minutes or until well done. 8. Serve fried cutlets with salsa on the side.

Zesty London Broil

Prep time: 30 minutes | Cook time: 20 to 28 minutes | Serves 4 to 6

160 ml ketchup	2 tablespoons minced onion
60 ml honey	½ teaspoon paprika
60 ml olive oil	1 teaspoon salt
2 tablespoons apple cider vinegar	1 teaspoon freshly ground black pepper
2 tablespoons Worcestershire sauce	900 g bavette or skirt steak (about 1-inch thick)

1. Combine the ketchup, honey, olive oil, apple cider vinegar, Worcestershire sauce, minced onion, paprika, salt and pepper in a small bowl and whisk together. 2. Generously pierce both sides of the meat with a fork or meat tenderizer and place it in a shallow dish. Pour the marinade mixture over the steak, making sure all sides of the meat get coated with the marinade. Cover and refrigerate overnight. 3. Preheat the air fryer to 204ºC. 4. Transfer the steak to the air fryer basket and cook for 20 to 28 minutes, depending on how rare or well done you like your steak. Flip the steak over halfway through the cooking time. 5. Remove the steak from the air fryer and let it rest for five minutes on a cutting board. To serve, thinly slice the meat against the grain and transfer to a serving platter.

Steaks with Walnut-Blue Cheese Butter

Prep time: 30 minutes | Cook time: 10 minutes | Serves 6

120 ml unsalted butter, at room temperature	1 teaspoon minced garlic
	¼ teaspoon cayenne pepper
120 ml crumbled blue cheese	Sea salt and freshly ground black pepper, to taste
2 tablespoons finely chopped walnuts	
	680 g sirloin steaks, at room temperature
1 tablespoon minced fresh rosemary	

1. In a medium bowl, combine the butter, blue cheese, walnuts, rosemary, garlic, and cayenne pepper and salt and black pepper to taste. Use clean hands to ensure that everything is well combined. Place the mixture on a sheet of parchment paper and form it into a log. Wrap it tightly in plastic wrap. Refrigerate for at least 2 hours or freeze for 30 minutes. 2. Season the steaks generously with salt and pepper. 3. Place the air fryer basket or grill pan in the air fryer. Set the air fryer to 204ºC and let it preheat for 5 minutes. 4. Place the steaks in the basket in a single layer and cook for 5 minutes. Flip the steaks, and cook for 5 minutes more, until an instant-read thermometer reads 49ºC for medium-rare (or as desired). 5. Transfer the steaks to a plate. Cut the butter into pieces and place the desired amount on top of the steaks. Tent a piece of aluminum foil over the steaks and allow to sit for 10 minutes before serving. 6. Store any remaining butter in a sealed container in the refrigerator for up to 2 weeks.

Greek-Style Meatloaf

Prep time: 5 minutes | Cook time: 25 minutes | Serves 6

450 g lean beef mince	1 teaspoon dried thyme
2 eggs	1 teaspoon salt
2 plum tomatoes, diced	1 teaspoon black pepper
½ brown onion, diced	60 g mozzarella cheese, shredded
120 ml whole wheat bread crumbs	
	1 tablespoon olive oil
1 teaspoon garlic powder	Fresh chopped parsley, for garnish
1 teaspoon dried oregano	

1. Preheat the oven to 192ºC. 2. In a large bowl, mix together the beef, eggs, tomatoes, onion, bread crumbs, garlic powder, oregano, thyme, salt, pepper, and cheese. 3. Form into a loaf, flattening to 1-inch thick. 4. Brush the top with olive oil, then place the meatloaf into the air fryer basket and cook for 25 minutes. 5. Remove from the air fryer and allow to rest for 5 minutes, before slicing and serving with a sprinkle of parsley.

Mexican Pork Chops

Prep time: 5 minutes | Cook time: 15 minutes | Serves 2

¼ teaspoon dried oregano

1½ teaspoons taco seasoning or fajita seasoning mix

2 (110 g) boneless pork chops

2 tablespoons unsalted butter, divided

1. Preheat the air fryer to 204ºC. 2. Combine the dried oregano and taco seasoning in a small bowl and rub the mixture into the pork chops. Brush the chops with 1 tablespoon butter. 3. In the air fryer, cook the chops for 15 minutes, turning them over halfway through to cook on the other side. 4. When the chops are a brown color, check the internal temperature has reached 64ºC and remove from the air fryer. Serve with a garnish of remaining butter.

Beef and Pork Sausage Meatloaf

Prep time: 20 minutes | Cook time: 25 minutes | Serves 4

340 g beef mince

110 g pork sausage meat

235 ml shallots, finely chopped

2 eggs, well beaten

3 tablespoons milk

1 tablespoon oyster sauce

1 teaspoon porcini mushrooms

½ teaspoon cumin powder

1 teaspoon garlic paste

1 tablespoon fresh parsley

Salt and crushed red pepper flakes, to taste

235 ml crushed cream crackers

Cooking spray

1. Preheat the air fryer to 182ºC. Spritz a baking dish with cooking spray. 2. Mix all the ingredients in a large bowl, combining everything well. 3. Transfer to the baking dish and cook in the air fryer for 25 minutes. 4. Serve hot.

Fruited Ham

Prep time: 15 minutes | Cook time: 8 to 10 minutes | Serves 4

235 ml orange marmalade

60 ml packed light brown sugar

¼ teaspoon ground cloves

½ teaspoon mustard powder

1 to 2 tablespoons oil

450 g cooked ham, cut into 1-inch cubes

120 ml canned mandarin oranges, drained and chopped

1. In a small bowl, stir together the orange marmalade, brown sugar, cloves, and mustard powder until blended. Set aside. 2. Preheat the air fryer to 160ºC. Spritz a baking pan with oil. 3. Place the ham cubes in the prepared pan. Pour the marmalade sauce over the ham to glaze it. 4. Cook for 4 minutes. Stir and cook for 2 minutes more. 5. Add the mandarin oranges and cook for 2 to 4 minutes more until the sauce begins to thicken and the ham is tender.

Cheesy Low-Carb Lasagna

Prep time: 10 minutes | Cook time: 10 minutes | Serves 4

Meat Layer:

Extra-virgin olive oil

450 g 85% lean beef mince

235 ml marinara sauce

60 ml diced celery

60 ml diced red onion

½ teaspoon minced garlic

Coarse or flaky salt and black pepper, to taste

Cheese Layer:

230 g ricotta cheese

235 ml shredded Mozzarella cheese

120 ml grated Parmesan cheese

2 large eggs

1 teaspoon dried Italian seasoning, crushed

½ teaspoon each minced garlic, garlic powder, and black pepper

1. For the meat layer: Grease a cake pan with 1 teaspoon olive oil. 2. In a large bowl, combine the beef mince, marinara, celery, onion, garlic, salt, and pepper. Place the seasoned meat in the pan. 3. Place the pan in the air fryer basket. Set the air fryer to 192ºC for 10 minutes. 4. Meanwhile, for the cheese layer: In a medium bowl, combine the ricotta, half the Mozzarella, the Parmesan, lightly beaten eggs, Italian seasoning, minced garlic, garlic powder, and pepper. Stir until well blended. 5. At the end of the cooking time, spread the cheese mixture over the meat mixture. Sprinkle with the remaining 120 ml Mozzarella. Set the air fryer to 192ºC for 10 minutes, or until the cheese is browned and bubbling. 6. At the end of the cooking time, use a meat thermometer to ensure the meat has reached an internal temperature of 72ºC. 7. Drain the fat and liquid from the pan. Let stand for 5 minutes before serving.

Rosemary Ribeye Steaks

Prep time: 10 minutes | Cook time: 15 minutes | Serves 2

60 ml butter

1 clove garlic, minced

Salt and ground black pepper, to taste

1½ tablespoons balsamic vinegar

60 ml rosemary, chopped

2 ribeye steaks

1. Melt the butter in a skillet over medium heat. Add the garlic and fry until fragrant. 2. Remove the skillet from the heat and add the salt, pepper, and vinegar. Allow it to cool. 3. Add the rosemary, then pour the mixture into a Ziploc bag. 4. Put the ribeye steaks in the bag and shake well, coating the meat well. Refrigerate for an hour, then allow to sit for a further twenty minutes. 5. Preheat the air fryer to 204ºC. 6. Cook the ribeye steaks for 15 minutes. 7. Take care when removing the steaks from the air fryer and plate up. 8. Serve immediately.

Mojito Lamb Chops

Prep time: 30 minutes | Cook time: 5 minutes | Serves 2

Marinade:
2 teaspoons grated lime zest
120 ml lime juice
60 ml avocado oil
60 ml chopped fresh mint leaves
4 cloves garlic, roughly chopped
2 teaspoons fine sea salt

½ teaspoon ground black pepper
4 (1-inch-thick) lamb chops
Sprigs of fresh mint, for garnish (optional)
Lime slices, for serving (optional)

1. Make the marinade: Place all the ingredients for the marinade in a food processor or blender and purée until mostly smooth with a few small chunks. Transfer half of the marinade to a shallow dish and set the other half aside for serving. Add the lamb to the shallow dish, cover, and place in the refrigerator to marinate for at least 2 hours or overnight. 2. Spray the air fryer basket with avocado oil. Preheat the air fryer to 200°C. 3. Remove the chops from the marinade and place them in the air fryer basket. Cook for 5 minutes, or until the internal temperature reaches 64°C for medium doneness. 4. Allow the chops to rest for 10 minutes before serving with the rest of the marinade as a sauce. Garnish with fresh mint leaves and serve with lime slices, if desired. Best served fresh.

Green Pepper Cheeseburgers

Prep time: 5 minutes | Cook time: 30 minutes | Serves 4

2 green peppers
680 g 85% lean beef mince
1 clove garlic, minced
1 teaspoon salt
½ teaspoon freshly ground black

pepper
4 slices Cheddar cheese (about 85 g)
4 large lettuce leaves

1. Preheat the air fryer to 204°C. 2. Arrange the peppers in the basket of the air fryer. Pausing halfway through the cooking time to turn the peppers, cook for 20 minutes, or until they are softened and beginning to char. Transfer the peppers to a large bowl and cover with a plate. When cool enough to handle, peel off the skin, remove the seeds and stems, and slice into strips. Set aside. 3. Meanwhile, in a large bowl, combine the beef with the garlic, salt, and pepper. Shape the beef into 4 patties. 4. Lower the heat on the air fryer to 182°C. Arrange the burgers in a single layer in the basket of the air fryer. Pausing halfway through the cooking time to turn the burgers, cook for 10 minutes, or until a thermometer inserted into the thickest part registers 72°C. 5. Top the burgers with the cheese slices and continue baking for a minute or two, just until the cheese has melted. Serve the burgers on a lettuce leaf topped with the roasted peppers.

Smothered Chops

Prep time: 20 minutes | Cook time: 30 minutes | Serves 4

4 bone-in pork chops (230 g each)
2 teaspoons salt, divided
1½ teaspoons freshly ground black pepper, divided
1 teaspoon garlic powder
235 ml tomato purée

1½ teaspoons Italian seasoning
1 tablespoon sugar
1 tablespoon cornflour
120 ml chopped onion
120 ml chopped green pepper
1 to 2 tablespoons oil

1. Evenly season the pork chops with 1 teaspoon salt, 1 teaspoon pepper, and the garlic powder. 2. In a medium bowl, stir together the tomato purée, Italian seasoning, sugar, remaining 1 teaspoon of salt, and remaining ½ teaspoon of pepper. 3. In a small bowl, whisk 180 ml water and the cornflour until blended. Stir this slurry into the tomato purée, with the onion and green pepper. Transfer to a baking pan. 4. Preheat the air fryer to 176°C. 5. Place the sauce in the fryer and cook for 10 minutes. Stir and cook for 10 minutes more. Remove the pan and keep warm. 6. Increase the air fryer temperature to 204°C. Line the air fryer basket with parchment paper. 7. Place the pork chops on the parchment and spritz with oil. 8. Cook for 5 minutes. Flip and spritz the chops with oil and cook for 5 minutes more, until the internal temperature reaches 64°C. Serve with the tomato mixture spooned on top.

Indian Mint and Chile Kebabs

Prep time: 30 minutes | Cook time: 15 minutes | Serves 4

450 g lamb mince
120 ml finely minced onion
60 ml chopped fresh mint
60 ml chopped fresh coriander
1 tablespoon minced garlic

½ teaspoon ground turmeric
½ teaspoon cayenne pepper
¼ teaspoon ground cardamom
¼ teaspoon ground cinnamon
1 teaspoon coarse or flaky salt

1. In the bowl of a stand mixer fitted with the paddle attachment, combine the lamb, onion, mint, coriander, garlic, turmeric, cayenne, cardamom, cinnamon, and salt. Mix on low speed until you have a sticky mess of spiced meat. If you have time, let the mixture stand at room temperature for 30 minutes (or cover and refrigerate for up to a day or two, until you're ready to make the kebabs). 2. Divide the meat into eight equal portions. Form each into a long sausage shape. Place the kebabs in a single layer in the air fryer basket. Set the air fryer to 176°C for 10 minutes. Increase the air fryer temperature to 204°C and cook for 3 to 4 minutes more to brown the kebabs. Use a meat thermometer to ensure the kebabs have reached an internal temperature of 72°C (medium).

Lamb Burger with Feta and Olives

Prep time: 10 minutes | Cook time: 20 minutes | Serves 3 to 4

2 teaspoons olive oil

⅓ onion, finely chopped

1 clove garlic, minced

450 g lamb mince

2 tablespoons fresh parsley, finely chopped

1½ teaspoons fresh oregano, finely chopped

120 ml black olives, finely chopped

80 ml crumbled feta cheese

½ teaspoon salt

Freshly ground black pepper, to taste

4 thick pitta breads

1. Preheat a medium skillet over medium-high heat on the stovetop. Add the olive oil and cook the onion until tender, but not browned, about 4 to 5 minutes. Add the garlic and cook for another minute. Transfer the onion and garlic to a mixing bowl and add the lamb mince, parsley, oregano, olives, feta cheese, salt and pepper. Gently mix the ingredients together. 2. Divide the mixture into 3 or 4 equal portions and then form the hamburgers, being careful not to over-handle the meat. One good way to do this is to throw the meat back and forth between your hands like a baseball, packing the meat each time you catch it. Flatten the balls into patties, making an indentation in the center of each patty. Flatten the sides of the patties as well to make it easier to fit them into the air fryer basket. 3. Preheat the air fryer to 188ºC. 4. If you don't have room for all four burgers, cook two or three burgers at a time for 8 minutes at 188ºC. Flip the burgers over and cook for another 8 minutes. If you cooked your burgers in batches, return the first batch of burgers to the air fryer for the last two minutes of cooking to re-heat. This should give you a medium-well burger. If you'd prefer a medium-rare burger, shorten the cooking time to about 13 minutes. Remove the burgers to a resting plate and let the burgers rest for a few minutes before dressing and serving. 5. While the burgers are resting, toast the pitta breads in the air fryer for 2 minutes. Tuck the burgers into the toasted pitta breads, or wrap the pittas around the burgers and serve with a tzatziki sauce or some mayonnaise.

Roast Beef with Horseradish Cream

Prep time: 5 minutes | Cook time: 35 to 45 minutes | Serves 6

900 g beef roasting joint

1 tablespoon salt

2 teaspoons garlic powder

1 teaspoon freshly ground black pepper

1 teaspoon dried thyme

Horseradish Cream:

80 ml double cream

80 ml sour cream

80 ml grated horseradish

2 teaspoons fresh lemon juice

Salt and freshly ground black pepper, to taste

1. Preheat the air fryer to 204ºC. 2. Season the beef with the salt, garlic powder, black pepper, and thyme. Place the beef fat-side down in the basket of the air fryer and lightly coat with olive oil. Pausing halfway through the cooking time to turn the meat, cook for 35 to 45 minutes, until a thermometer inserted into the thickest part indicates the desired doneness, 52ºC (rare) to 64ºC (medium). Let the beef rest for 10 minutes before slicing. 3. To make the horseradish cream: In a small bowl, combine the double cream, sour cream, horseradish, and lemon juice. Whisk until thoroughly combined. Season to taste with salt and freshly ground black pepper. Serve alongside the beef.

Chorizo and Beef Burger

Prep time: 10 minutes | Cook time: 15 minutes | Serves 4

340 g 80/20 beef mince

110 g Mexican-style chorizo crumb

60 ml chopped onion

5 slices pickled jalapeños,

chopped

2 teaspoons chili powder

1 teaspoon minced garlic

¼ teaspoon cumin

1. In a large bowl, mix all ingredients. Divide the mixture into four sections and form them into burger patties. 2. Place burger patties into the air fryer basket, working in batches if necessary. 3. Adjust the temperature to 192ºC and cook for 15 minutes. 4. Flip the patties halfway through the cooking time. Serve warm.

Pork Chops with Caramelized Onions

Prep time: 20 minutes | Cook time: 23 to 34 minutes | Serves 4

4 bone-in pork chops (230 g each)

1 to 2 tablespoons oil

2 tablespoons Cajun seasoning,

divided

1 brown onion, thinly sliced

1 green pepper, thinly sliced

2 tablespoons light brown sugar

1. Spritz the pork chops with oil. Sprinkle 1 tablespoon of Cajun seasoning on one side of the chops. 2. Preheat the air fryer to 204ºC. Line the air fryer basket with parchment paper and spritz the parchment with oil. 3. Place 2 pork chops, spice-side up, on the paper. 4. Cook for 4 minutes. Flip the chops, sprinkle with the remaining 1 tablespoon of Cajun seasoning, and cook for 4 to 8 minutes more until the internal temperature reaches 64ºC, depending on the chops' thickness. Remove and keep warm while you cook the remaining 2 chops. Set the chops aside. 5. In a baking pan, combine the onion, pepper, and brown sugar, stirring until the vegetables are coated. Place the pan in the air fryer basket and cook for 4 minutes. 6. Stir the vegetables. Cook for 3 to 6 minutes more to your desired doneness. Spoon the vegetable mixture over the chops to serve.

Mustard Lamb Chops

Prep time: 5 minutes | Cook time: 14 minutes | Serves 4

Oil, for spraying
1 tablespoon Dijon mustard
2 teaspoons lemon juice
½ teaspoon dried tarragon
¼ teaspoon salt

¼ teaspoon freshly ground black pepper
4 (1¼-inch-thick) loin lamb chops

1. Preheat the air fryer to 200°C. Line the air fryer basket with parchment and spray lightly with oil. 2. In a small bowl, mix together the mustard, lemon juice, tarragon, salt, and black pepper. 3. Pat dry the lamb chops with a paper towel. Brush the chops on both sides with the mustard mixture. 4. Place the chops in the prepared basket. You may need to work in batches, depending on the size of your air fryer. 5. Cook for 8 minutes, flip, and cook for another 6 minutes, or until the internal temperature reaches 52°C for rare, 64°C for medium-rare, or 68°C for medium.

Currywurst

Prep time: 15 minutes | Cook time: 12 minutes | Serves 4

235 ml tomato sauce
2 tablespoons cider vinegar
2 teaspoons curry powder
2 teaspoons sweet paprika
1 teaspoon sugar

¼ teaspoon cayenne pepper
1 small onion, diced
450 g bratwurst, sliced diagonally into 1-inch pieces

1. In a large bowl, combine the tomato sauce, vinegar, curry powder, paprika, sugar, and cayenne. Whisk until well combined. Stir in the onion and bratwurst. 2. Transfer the mixture to a baking pan. Place the pan in the air fryer basket. Set the air fryer to 204°C for 12 minutes, or until the sausage is heated through and the sauce is bubbling.

Southern Chili

Prep time: 20 minutes | Cook time: 25 minutes | Serves 4

450 g beef mince (85% lean)
235 ml minced onion
1 (794 g) can tomato purée
1 (425 g) can diced tomatoes

1 (425 g) can red kidney beans, rinsed and drained
60 ml Chili seasoning

1. Preheat the air fryer to 204°C. 2. In a baking pan, mix the mince and onion. Place the pan in the air fryer. 3. Cook for 4 minutes. Stir and cook for 4 minutes more until browned. Remove the pan from the fryer. Drain the meat and transfer to a large bowl. 4. Reduce the air fryer temperature to 176°C. 5. To the bowl with the meat, add in the tomato purée, diced tomatoes, kidney beans, and Chili seasoning. Mix well. Pour the mixture into the baking pan. 6. Cook for 25 minutes, stirring every 10 minutes, until thickened.

Sausage and Peppers

Prep time: 7 minutes | Cook time: 35 minutes | Serves 4

Oil, for spraying
900 g hot or sweet Italian-seasoned sausage links, cut into thick slices
4 large peppers of any color, seeded and cut into slices
1 onion, thinly sliced

1 tablespoon olive oil
1 tablespoon chopped fresh parsley
1 teaspoon dried oregano
1 teaspoon dried basil
1 teaspoon balsamic vinegar

1. Line the air fryer basket with parchment and spray lightly with oil. 2. In a large bowl, combine the sausage, peppers, and onion. 3. In a small bowl, whisk together the olive oil, parsley, oregano, basil, and balsamic vinegar. Pour the mixture over the sausage and peppers and toss until evenly coated. 4. Using a slotted spoon, transfer the mixture to the prepared basket, taking care to drain out as much excess liquid as possible. 5. Cook at 176°C for 20 minutes, stir, and cook for another 15 minutes, or until the sausage is browned and the juices run clear.

Bone-in Pork Chops

Prep time: 5 minutes | Cook time: 10 to 12 minutes | Serves 2

450 g bone-in pork chops
1 tablespoon avocado oil
1 teaspoon smoked paprika
½ teaspoon onion granules

¼ teaspoon cayenne pepper
Sea salt and freshly ground black pepper, to taste

1. Brush the pork chops with the avocado oil. In a small dish, mix together the smoked paprika, onion granules, cayenne pepper, and salt and black pepper to taste. Sprinkle the seasonings over both sides of the pork chops. 2. Set the air fryer to 204°C. Place the chops in the air fryer basket in a single layer, working in batches if necessary. Cook for 10 to 12 minutes, until an instant-read thermometer reads 64°C at the chops' thickest point. 3. Remove the chops from the air fryer and allow them to rest for 5 minutes before serving.

Greek Lamb Rack

Prep time: 5 minutes | Cook time: 10 minutes | Serves 4

60 ml freshly squeezed lemon juice

1 teaspoon oregano

2 teaspoons minced fresh rosemary

1 teaspoon minced fresh thyme

2 tablespoons minced garlic

Salt and freshly ground black pepper, to taste

2 to 4 tablespoons olive oil

1 lamb rib rack (7 to 8 ribs)

1. Preheat the air fryer to 182°C. 2. In a small mixing bowl, combine the lemon juice, oregano, rosemary, thyme, garlic, salt, pepper, and olive oil and mix well. 3. Rub the mixture over the lamb, covering all the meat. Put the rack of lamb in the air fryer. Cook for 10 minutes. Flip the rack halfway through. 4. After 10 minutes, measure the internal temperature of the rack of lamb reaches at least 64°C. 5. Serve immediately.

Deef and Tomato Sauce Meatloaf

Prep time: 15 minutes | Cook time: 25 minutes | Serves 4

680 g beef mince

235 ml tomato sauce

120 ml breadcrumbs

2 egg whites

120 ml grated Parmesan cheese

1 diced onion

2 tablespoons chopped parsley

2 tablespoons minced ginger

2 garlic cloves, minced

½ teaspoon dried basil

1 teaspoon cayenne pepper

Salt and ground black pepper, to taste

Cooking spray

1. Preheat the air fryer to 182°C. Spritz a meatloaf pan with cooking spray. 2. Combine all the ingredients in a large bowl. Stir to mix well. 3. Pour the meat mixture in the prepared meatloaf pan and press with a spatula to make it firm. 4. Arrange the pan in the preheated air fryer and cook for 25 minutes or until the beef is well browned. 5. Serve immediately.

Beef Burger

Prep time: 20 minutes | Cook time: 12 minutes | Serves 4

570 g lean beef mince

1 tablespoon soy sauce or tamari

1 teaspoon Dijon mustard

1/2 teaspoon smoked paprika

1 teaspoon shallot powder

1 clove garlic, minced

½ teaspoon cumin powder

60 ml spring onions, minced

⅓ teaspoon sea salt flakes

⅓ teaspoon freshly cracked mixed peppercorns

1 teaspoon celery salt

1 teaspoon dried parsley

1. Mix all of the above ingredients in a bowl; knead until everything is well incorporated. 2. Shape the mixture into four patties. Next, make a shallow dip in the center of each patty to prevent them puffing up during air frying. 3. Spritz the patties on all sides using nonstick cooking spray. Cook approximately 12 minutes at 182°C. 4. Check for doneness, an instant-read thermometer should read 72°C. Bon appétit!

Garlic Balsamic London Broil

Prep time: 30 minutes | Cook time: 8 to 10 minutes | Serves 8

900 g bavette or skirt steak

3 large garlic cloves, minced

3 tablespoons balsamic vinegar

3 tablespoons wholegrain mustard

2 tablespoons olive oil

Sea salt and ground black pepper, to taste

½ teaspoon dried hot red pepper flakes

1. Score both sides of the cleaned steak. 2. Thoroughly combine the remaining ingredients; massage this mixture into the meat to coat it on all sides. Let it marinate for at least 3 hours. 3. Set the air fryer to 204°C; Then cook the steak for 15 minutes. Flip it over and cook another 10 to 12 minutes. Bon appétit!

Chapter 5 Poultry

Chapter 5 Poultry

Chicken Pesto Parmigiana

Prep time: 10 minutes | Cook time: 23 minutes | Serves 4

2 large eggs	pounded to ¼ inch thick
1 tablespoon water	65 g pesto
Fine sea salt and ground black pepper, to taste	115 g shredded Mozzarella cheese
85 g powdered Parmesan cheese	Finely chopped fresh basil, for garnish (optional)
2 teaspoons Italian seasoning	Grape tomatoes, halved, for serving (optional)
4 (140 g) boneless, skinless chicken breasts or thighs,	

1. Spray the air fryer basket with avocado oil. Preheat the air fryer to 200°C. 2. Crack the eggs into a shallow baking dish, add the water and a pinch each of salt and pepper, and whisk to combine. In another shallow baking dish, stir together the Parmesan and Italian seasoning until well combined. 3. Season the chicken breasts well on both sides with salt and pepper. Dip one chicken breast in the eggs and let any excess drip off, then dredge both sides of the breast in the Parmesan mixture. Spray the breast with avocado oil and place it in the air fryer basket. Repeat with the remaining 3 chicken breasts. 4. Cook the chicken in the air fryer for 20 minutes, or until the internal temperature reaches 76°C and the breading is golden brown, flipping halfway through. 5. Dollop each chicken breast with ¼ of the pesto and top with the Mozzarella. Return the breasts to the air fryer and cook for 3 minutes, or until the cheese is melted. Garnish with basil and serve with halved grape tomatoes on the side, if desired. 6. Store leftovers in an airtight container in the refrigerator for up to 4 days. Reheat in a preheated 200°C air fryer for 5 minutes, or until warmed through.

Apricot-Glazed Chicken Drumsticks

Prep time: 15 minutes | Cook time: 30 minutes | Makes 6 drumsticks

For the Glaze:	6 chicken drumsticks
160 g apricot preserves	½ teaspoon seasoning salt
½ teaspoon tamari	1 teaspoon salt
¼ teaspoon chili powder	½ teaspoon ground black pepper
2 teaspoons Dijon mustard	Cooking spray
For the Chicken:	

Make the glaze: 1. Combine the ingredients for the glaze in a saucepan, then heat over low heat for 10 minutes or until thickened. 2. Turn off the heat and sit until ready to use. Make the Chicken:

1. Preheat the air fryer to 190°C. Spritz the air fryer basket with cooking spray. 2. Combine the seasoning salt, salt, and pepper in a small bowl. Stir to mix well. 3. Place the chicken drumsticks in the preheated air fryer. Spritz with cooking spray and sprinkle with the salt mixture on both sides. 4. Cook for 20 minutes or until well browned. Flip the chicken halfway through. 5. Baste the chicken with the glaze and air fryer for 2 more minutes or until the chicken tenderloin is glossy. 6. Serve immediately.

Lemon Chicken with Garlic

Prep time: 5 minutes | Cook time: 20 to 25 minutes | Serves 4

8 bone-in chicken thighs, skin on	½ teaspoon paprika
	½ teaspoon garlic powder
1 tablespoon olive oil	¼ teaspoon freshly ground black pepper
1½ teaspoons lemon-pepper seasoning	Juice of ½ lemon

1. Preheat the air fryer to 180°C. 2. Place the chicken in a large bowl and drizzle with the olive oil. Top with the lemon-pepper seasoning, paprika, garlic powder, and freshly ground black pepper. Toss until thoroughly coated. 3. Working in batches if necessary, arrange the chicken in a single layer in the basket of the air fryer. Pausing halfway through the cooking time to turn the chicken, cook for 20 to 25 minutes, until a thermometer inserted into the thickest piece registers 76°C. 4. Transfer the chicken to a serving platter and squeeze the lemon juice over the top.

Pecan-Crusted Chicken Tenders

Prep time: 10 minutes | Cook time: 12 minutes | Serves 4

2 tablespoons mayonnaise	½ teaspoon salt
1 teaspoon Dijon mustard	¼ teaspoon ground black pepper
455 g boneless, skinless chicken tenders	75 g chopped roasted pecans, finely ground

1. In a small bowl, whisk mayonnaise and mustard until combined. Brush mixture onto chicken tenders on both sides, then sprinkle tenders with salt and pepper. 2. Place pecans in a medium bowl and press each tender into pecans to coat each side. 3. Place tenders into ungreased air fryer basket in a single layer, working in batches if needed. Adjust the temperature to (190°C and cook for 12 minutes, turning tenders halfway through cooking. Tenders will be golden brown and have an internal temperature of at least 76°C when done. Serve warm.

African Piri-Piri Chicken Drumsticks

Prep time: 30 minutes | Cook time: 20 minutes | Serves 2

Chicken:
1 tablespoon chopped fresh thyme leaves
1 tablespoon minced fresh ginger
1 small shallot, finely chopped
2 garlic cloves, minced
80 ml piri-piri sauce or hot sauce
3 tablespoons extra-virgin olive oil
Zest and juice of 1 lemon

1 teaspoon smoked paprika
½ teaspoon kosher salt
½ teaspoon black pepper
4 chicken drumsticks
Glaze:
2 tablespoons butter or ghee
1 teaspoon chopped fresh thyme leaves
1 garlic clove, minced
1 tablespoon piri-piri sauce
1 tablespoon fresh lemon juice

1. For the chicken: In a small bowl, stir together all the ingredients except the chicken. Place the chicken and the marinade in a gallon-size resealable plastic bag. Seal the bag and massage to coat. Refrigerate for at least 2 hours or up to 24 hours, turning the bag occasionally. 2. Place the chicken legs in the air fryer basket. Set the air fryer to 200ºC for 20 minutes, turning the chicken halfway through the cooking time. 3. Meanwhile, for the glaze: Melt the butter in a small saucepan over medium-high heat. Add the thyme and garlic. Cook, stirring, until the garlic just begins to brown, 1 to 2 minutes. Add the piri-piri sauce and lemon juice. Reduce the heat to medium-low and simmer for 1 to 2 minutes. 4. Transfer the chicken to a serving platter. Pour the glaze over the chicken. Serve immediately.

African Merguez Meatballs

Prep time: 30 minutes | Cook time: 10 minutes | Serves 4

450 g chicken mince
2 garlic cloves, finely minced
1 tablespoon sweet Hungarian paprika
1 teaspoon kosher salt
1 teaspoon sugar

1 teaspoon ground cumin
½ teaspoon black pepper
½ teaspoon ground fennel
½ teaspoon ground coriander
½ teaspoon cayenne pepper
¼ teaspoon ground allspice

1. In a large bowl, gently mix the chicken, garlic, paprika, salt, sugar, cumin, black pepper, fennel, coriander, cayenne, and allspice until all the ingredients are incorporated. Let stand for 30 minutes at room temperature, or cover and refrigerate for up to 24 hours. 2. Form the mixture into 16 meatballs. Arrange them in a single layer in the air fryer basket. Set the air fryer to 200ºC for 10 minutes, turning the meatballs halfway through the cooking time. Use a meat thermometer to ensure the meatballs have reached an internal temperature of 76ºC.

Porchetta-Style Chicken Breasts

Prep time: 10 minutes | Cook time: 15 minutes | Serves 4

25 g fresh parsley leaves
10 g roughly chopped fresh chives
4 cloves garlic, peeled
2 tablespoons lemon juice
3 teaspoons fine sea salt
1 teaspoon dried rubbed sage
1 teaspoon fresh rosemary leaves

1 teaspoon ground fennel
½ teaspoon red pepper flakes
4 (115 g) boneless, skinless chicken breasts, pounded to ¼ inch thick
8 slices bacon
Sprigs of fresh rosemary, for garnish (optional)

1. Spray the air fryer basket with avocado oil. Preheat the air fryer to 170ºC. 2. Place the parsley, chives, garlic, lemon juice, salt, sage, rosemary, fennel, and red pepper flakes in a food processor and purée until a smooth paste forms. 3. Place the chicken breasts on a cutting board and rub the paste all over the tops. With a short end facing you, roll each breast up like a jelly roll to make a log and secure it with toothpicks. 4. Wrap 2 slices of bacon around each chicken breast log to cover the entire breast. Secure the bacon with toothpicks. 5. Place the chicken breast logs in the air fryer basket and cook for 5 minutes, flip the logs over, and cook for another 5 minutes. Increase the heat to 200ºC and cook until the bacon is crisp, about 5 minutes more. 6. Remove the toothpicks and garnish with fresh rosemary sprigs, if desired, before serving. Store leftovers in an airtight container in the refrigerator for up to 4 days or in the freezer for up to a month. Reheat in a preheated 180ºC air fryer for 5 minutes, then increase the heat to 200ºC and cook for 2 minutes to crisp the bacon.

Cajun-Breaded Chicken Bites

Prep time: 10 minutes | Cook time: 12 minutes | Serves 4

450 g boneless, skinless chicken breasts, cut into 1-inch cubes
120 g heavy whipping cream
½ teaspoon salt
¼ teaspoon ground black pepper

30 g plain pork rinds, finely crushed
40 g unflavoured whey protein powder
½ teaspoon Cajun seasoning

1. Place chicken in a medium bowl and pour in cream. Stir to coat. Sprinkle with salt and pepper. 2. In a separate large bowl, combine pork rinds, protein powder, and Cajun seasoning. Remove chicken from cream, shaking off any excess, and toss in dry mix until fully coated. 3. Place bites into ungreased air fryer basket. Adjust the temperature to 200ºC and cook for 12 minutes, shaking the basket twice during cooking. Bites will be done when golden brown and have an internal temperature of at least 76ºC. Serve warm.

Chicken Breasts with Asparagus, Beans, and Rocket

Prep time: 20 minutes | Cook time: 25 minutes | Serves 2

160 g canned cannellini beans, rinsed

1½ tablespoons red wine vinegar

1 garlic clove, minced

2 tablespoons extra-virgin olive oil, divided

Salt and ground black pepper, to taste

½ red onion, sliced thinly

230 g asparagus, trimmed and cut into 1-inch lengths

2 (230 g) boneless, skinless chicken breasts, trimmed

¼ teaspoon paprika

½ teaspoon ground coriander

60 g baby rocket, rinsed and drained

1. Preheat the air fryer to 200ºC. 2. Warm the beans in microwave for 1 minutes and combine with red wine vinegar, garlic, 1 tablespoon of olive oil, ¼ teaspoon of salt, and ¼ teaspoon of ground black pepper in a bowl. Stir to mix well. 3. Combine the onion with ⅛ teaspoon of salt, ⅛ teaspoon of ground black pepper, and 2 teaspoons of olive oil in a separate bowl. Toss to coat well. 4. Place the onion in the air fryer and cook for 2 minutes, then add the asparagus and cook for 8 more minutes or until the asparagus is tender. Shake the basket halfway through. Transfer the onion and asparagus to the bowl with beans. Set aside. 5. Toss the chicken breasts with remaining ingredients, except for the baby rocket, in a large bowl. 6. Put the chicken breasts in the air fryer and cook for 14 minutes or until the internal temperature of the chicken reaches at least 76ºC. Flip the breasts halfway through. 7. Remove the chicken from the air fryer and serve on an aluminum foil with asparagus, beans, onion, and rocket. Sprinkle with salt and ground black pepper. Toss to serve.

Coriander Lime Chicken Thighs

Prep time: 15 minutes | Cook time: 22 minutes | Serves 4

4 bone-in, skin-on chicken thighs

1 teaspoon baking powder

½ teaspoon garlic powder

2 teaspoons chili powder

1 teaspoon cumin

2 medium limes

5 g chopped fresh coriander

1. Pat chicken thighs dry and sprinkle with baking powder. 2. In a small bowl, mix garlic powder, chili powder, and cumin and sprinkle evenly over thighs, gently rubbing on and under chicken skin. 3. Cut one lime in half and squeeze juice over thighs. Place chicken into the air fryer basket. 4. Adjust the temperature to 190ºC and cook for 22 minutes. 5. Cut other lime into four wedges for serving and garnish cooked chicken with wedges and coriander.

Ethiopian Chicken with Cauliflower

Prep time: 15 minutes | Cook time: 28 minutes | Serves 6

2 handful fresh Italian parsley, roughly chopped

20 g fresh chopped chives

2 sprigs thyme

6 chicken drumsticks

1½ small-sized head cauliflower, broken into large-sized florets

2 teaspoons mustard powder

⅓ teaspoon porcini powder

1½ teaspoons berbere spice

⅓ teaspoon sweet paprika

½ teaspoon shallot powder

1teaspoon granulated garlic

1 teaspoon freshly cracked pink peppercorns

½ teaspoon sea salt

1. Simply combine all items for the berbere spice rub mix. After that, coat the chicken drumsticks with this rub mix on all sides. Transfer them to the baking dish. 2. Now, lower the cauliflower onto the chicken drumsticks. Add thyme, chives and Italian parsley and spritz everything with a pan spray. Transfer the baking dish to the preheated air fryer. 3. Next step, set the timer for 28 minutes; cook at 180ºC, turning occasionally. Bon appétit!

Broccoli Cheese Chicken

Prep time: 15 minutes | Cook time: 25 minutes | Serves 4

1 tablespoon avocado oil

15 g chopped onion

35 g finely chopped broccoli

115 g cream cheese, at room temperature

60 g Cheddar cheese, shredded

1 teaspoon garlic powder

½ teaspoon sea salt, plus

additional for seasoning, divided

¼ freshly ground black pepper, plus additional for seasoning, divided

900 g boneless, skinless chicken breasts

1 teaspoon smoked paprika

1. Heat a medium skillet over medium-high heat and pour in the avocado oil. Add the onion and broccoli and cook, stirring occasionally, for 5 to 8 minutes, until the onion is tender. 2. Transfer to a large bowl and stir in the cream cheese, Cheddar cheese, and garlic powder, and season to taste with salt and pepper. 3. Hold a sharp knife parallel to the chicken breast and cut a long pocket into one side. Stuff the chicken pockets with the broccoli mixture, using toothpicks to secure the pockets around the filling. 4. In a small dish, combine the paprika, ½ teaspoon salt, and ¼ teaspoon pepper. Sprinkle this over the outside of the chicken. 5. Set the air fryer to 200ºC. Place the chicken in a single layer in the air fryer basket, cooking in batches if necessary, and cook for 14 to 16 minutes, until an instant-read thermometer reads 70ºC. Place the chicken on a plate and tent a piece of aluminum foil over the chicken. Allow to rest for 5 to 10 minutes before serving.

Spice-Rubbed Turkey Breast

Prep time: 5 minutes | Cook time: 45 to 55 minutes | Serves 10

1 tablespoon sea salt	pepper
1 teaspoon paprika	1.8 kg bone-in, skin-on turkey
1 teaspoon onion powder	breast
1 teaspoon garlic powder	2 tablespoons unsalted butter,
½ teaspoon freshly ground black	melted

1. In a small bowl, combine the salt, paprika, onion powder, garlic powder, and pepper. 2. Sprinkle the seasonings all over the turkey. Brush the turkey with some of the melted butter. 3. Set the air fryer to 180°C. . Place the turkey in the air fryer basket, skin-side down, and cook for 25 minutes. 4. Flip the turkey and brush it with the remaining butter. Continue cooking for another 20 to 30 minutes, until an instant-read thermometer reads 70°C. 5. Remove the turkey breast from the air fryer. Tent a piece of aluminum foil over the turkey, and allow it to rest for about 5 minutes before serving.

Easy Cajun Chicken Drumsticks

Prep time: 5 minutes | Cook time: 40 minutes | Serves 5

1 tablespoon olive oil	Salt and ground black pepper, to
10 chicken drumsticks	taste
1½ tablespoons Cajun seasoning	

1. Preheat the air fryer to 200°C. Grease the air fryer basket with olive oil. 2. On a clean work surface, rub the chicken drumsticks with Cajun seasoning, salt, and ground black pepper. 3. Arrange the seasoned chicken drumsticks in a single layer in the air fryer. You need to work in batches to avoid overcrowding. 4. Cook for 18 minutes or until lightly browned. Flip the drumsticks halfway through. 5. Remove the chicken drumsticks from the air fryer. Serve immediately.

Bruschetta Chicken

Prep time: 10 minutes | Cook time: 20 minutes | Serves 4

Bruschetta Stuffing:	oil
1 tomato, diced	Chicken:
3 tablespoons balsamic vinegar	4 (115 g) boneless, skinless
1 teaspoon Italian seasoning	chicken breasts, cut 4 slits each
2 tablespoons chopped fresh	1 teaspoon Italian seasoning
basil	Chicken seasoning or rub, to
3 garlic cloves, minced	taste
2 tablespoons extra-virgin olive	Cooking spray

1. Preheat the air fryer to 190°. Spritz the air fryer basket with cooking spray. 2. Combine the ingredients for the bruschetta stuffing in a bowl. Stir to mix well. Set aside. 3. Rub the chicken breasts with Italian seasoning and chicken seasoning on a clean work surface. 4. Arrange the chicken breasts, slits side up, in a single layer in the air fryer basket and spritz with cooking spray. You may need to work in batches to avoid overcrowding. 5. Cook for 7 minutes, then open the air fryer and fill the slits in the chicken with the bruschetta stuffing. Cook for another 3 minutes or until the chicken is well browned. 6. Serve immediately.

Thai Chicken with Cucumber and Chili Salad

Prep time: 25 minutes | Cook time: 25 minutes | Serves 6

2 (570 g) small chickens, giblets	taste
discarded	1 English cucumber, halved
1 tablespoon fish sauce	lengthwise and sliced thin
6 tablespoons chopped fresh	1 Thai chili, stemmed, deseeded,
coriander	and minced
2 teaspoons lime zest	2 tablespoons chopped dry-
1 teaspoon ground coriander	roasted peanuts
2 garlic cloves, minced	1 small shallot, sliced thinly
2 tablespoons packed light	1 tablespoon lime juice
brown sugar	Lime wedges, for serving
2 teaspoons vegetable oil	Cooking spray
Salt and ground black pepper, to	

1. Arrange a chicken on a clean work surface, remove the backbone with kitchen shears, then pound the chicken breast to flat. Cut the breast in half. Repeat with the remaining chicken. 2. Loose the breast and thigh skin with your fingers, then pat the chickens dry and pierce about 10 holes into the fat deposits of the chickens. Tuck the wings under the chickens. 3. Combine 2 teaspoons of fish sauce, coriander, lime zest, coriander, garlic, 4 teaspoons of sugar, 1 teaspoon of vegetable oil, ½ teaspoon of salt, and ⅛ teaspoon of ground black pepper in a small bowl. Stir to mix well. 4. Rub the fish sauce mixture under the breast and thigh skin of the game chickens, then let sit for 10 minutes to marinate. 5. Preheat the air fryer to 200°C. Spritz the air fryer basket with cooking spray. 6. Arrange the marinated chickens in the preheated air fryer, skin side down. 7. Cook for 15 minutes, then gently turn the game hens over and cook for 10 more minutes or until the skin is golden brown and the internal temperature of the chickens reads at least 76°C. 8. Meanwhile, combine all the remaining ingredients, except for the lime wedges, in a large bowl and sprinkle with salt and black pepper. Toss to mix well. 9. Transfer the fried chickens on a large plate, then sit the salad aside and squeeze the lime wedges over before serving.

Gold Livers

Prep time: 10 minutes | Cook time: 20 minutes | Serves 4

2 eggs
2 tablespoons water
90 g flour
240 g panko breadcrumbs
1 teaspoon salt
½ teaspoon ground black pepper
570 g chicken livers
Cooking spray

1. Preheat the air fryer to 200ºC. Spritz the air fryer basket with cooking spray. 2. Whisk the eggs with water in a large bowl. Pour the flour in a separate bowl. Pour the panko on a shallow dish and sprinkle with salt and pepper. 3. Dredge the chicken livers in the flour. Shake the excess off, then dunk the livers in the whisked eggs, and then roll the livers over the panko to coat well. 4. Arrange the livers in the preheated air fryer and spritz with cooking spray. Work in batches to avoid overcrowding. 5. Cook for 10 minutes or until the livers are golden and crispy. Flip the livers halfway through. Repeat with remaining livers. 6. Serve immediately.

Air Fried Chicken Potatoes with Sun-Dried Tomato

Prep time: 15 minutes | Cook time: 25 minutes | Serves 2

2 teaspoons minced fresh oregano, divided
2 teaspoons minced fresh thyme, divided
2 teaspoons extra-virgin olive oil, plus extra as needed
450 g fingerling potatoes, unpeeled
2 (340 g) bone-in split chicken breasts, trimmed
1 garlic clove, minced
15 g oil-packed sun-dried tomatoes, patted dry and chopped
1½ tablespoons red wine vinegar
1 tablespoon capers, rinsed and minced
1 small shallot, minced
Salt and ground black pepper, to taste

1. Preheat the air fryer to 180ºC. 2. Combine 1 teaspoon of oregano, 1 teaspoon of thyme, ¼ teaspoon of salt, ¼ teaspoon of ground black pepper, 1 teaspoons of olive oil in a large bowl. Add the potatoes and toss to coat well. 3. Combine the chicken with remaining thyme, oregano, and olive oil. Sprinkle with garlic, salt, and pepper. Toss to coat well. 4. Place the potatoes in the preheated air fryer, then arrange the chicken on top of the potatoes. 5. Cook for 25 minutes or until the internal temperature of the chicken reaches at least 76ºC and the potatoes are wilted. Flip the chicken and potatoes halfway through. 6. Meanwhile, combine the sun-dried tomatoes, vinegar, capers, and shallot in a separate large bowl. Sprinkle with salt and ground black pepper. Toss to mix well. 7. Remove the chicken and potatoes from the air fryer and allow to cool for 10 minutes. Serve with the sun-dried tomato mix.

Chicken Hand Pies

Prep time: 30 minutes | Cook time: 10 minutes per batch | Makes 8 pies

180 ml chicken broth
130 g frozen mixed peas and carrots
140 g cooked chicken, chopped
1 tablespoon cornflour
1 tablespoon milk
Salt and pepper, to taste
1 (8-count) can organic flaky biscuits
Oil for misting or cooking spray

1. In a medium saucepan, bring chicken broth to a boil. Stir in the frozen peas and carrots and cook for 5 minutes over medium heat. Stir in chicken. 2. Mix the cornflour into the milk until it dissolves. Stir it into the simmering chicken broth mixture and cook just until thickened. 3. Remove from heat, add salt and pepper to taste, and let cool slightly. 4. Lay biscuits out on wax paper. Peel each biscuit apart in the middle to make 2 rounds so you have 16 rounds total. Using your hands or a rolling pin, flatten each biscuit round slightly to make it larger and thinner. 5. Divide chicken filling among 8 of the biscuit rounds. Place remaining biscuit rounds on top and press edges all around. Use the tines of a fork to crimp biscuit edges and make sure they are sealed well. 6. Spray both sides lightly with oil or cooking spray. 7. Cook in a single layer, 4 at a time, at 170ºC for 10 minutes or until biscuit dough is cooked through and golden brown.

Buttermilk-Fried Drumsticks

Prep time: 10 minutes | Cook time: 25 minutes | Serves 2

1 egg
120 g buttermilk
90 g self-rising flour
90 g seasoned panko bread crumbs
1 teaspoon salt
¼ teaspoon ground black pepper (to mix into coating)
4 chicken drumsticks, skin on
Oil for misting or cooking spray

1. Beat together egg and buttermilk in shallow dish. 2. In a second shallow dish, combine the flour, panko crumbs, salt, and pepper. 3. Sprinkle chicken legs with additional salt and pepper to taste. 4. Dip legs in buttermilk mixture, then roll in panko mixture, pressing in crumbs to make coating stick. Mist with oil or cooking spray. 5. Spray the air fryer basket with cooking spray. 6. Cook drumsticks at 180ºC for 10 minutes. Turn pieces over and cook an additional 10 minutes. 7. Turn pieces to check for browning. If you have any white spots that haven't begun to brown, spritz them with oil or cooking spray. Continue cooking for 5 more minutes or until crust is golden brown and juices run clear. Larger, meatier drumsticks will take longer to cook than small ones.

Pomegranate-Glazed Chicken with Couscous Salad

Prep time: 25 minutes | Cook time: 20 minutes | Serves 4

3 tablespoons plus 2 teaspoons pomegranate molasses
½ teaspoon ground cinnamon
1 teaspoon minced fresh thyme
Salt and ground black pepper, to taste
2 (340 g) bone-in split chicken breasts, trimmed
60 ml chicken broth
60 ml water
80 g couscous
1 tablespoon minced fresh parsley
60 g cherry tomatoes, quartered
1 scallion, white part minced, green part sliced thin on bias
1 tablespoon extra-virgin olive oil
30 g feta cheese, crumbled
Cooking spray

1. Preheat the air fryer to 180ºC. Spritz the air fryer basket with cooking spray. 2. Combine 3 tablespoons of pomegranate molasses, cinnamon, thyme, and ⅛ teaspoon of salt in a small bowl. Stir to mix well. Set aside. 3. Place the chicken breasts in the preheated air fryer, skin side down, and spritz with cooking spray. Sprinkle with salt and ground black pepper. 4. Cook the chicken for 10 minutes, then brush the chicken with half of pomegranate molasses mixture and flip. Cook for 5 more minutes. 5. Brush the chicken with remaining pomegranate molasses mixture and flip. Cook for another 5 minutes or until the internal temperature of the chicken breasts reaches at least 76ºC. 6. Meanwhile, pour the broth and water in a pot and bring to a boil over medium-high heat. Add the couscous and sprinkle with salt. Cover and simmer for 7 minutes or until the liquid is almost absorbed. 7. Combine the remaining ingredients, except for the cheese, with cooked couscous in a large bowl. Toss to mix well. Scatter with the feta cheese. 8. When the air frying is complete, remove the chicken from the air fryer and allow to cool for 10 minutes. Serve with vegetable and couscous salad.

Harissa-Rubbed Chicken

Prep time: 30 minutes | Cook time: 21 minutes | Serves 4

Harissa:
120 ml olive oil
6 cloves garlic, minced
2 tablespoons smoked paprika
1 tablespoon ground coriander
1 tablespoon ground cumin
1 teaspoon ground caraway
1 teaspoon kosher salt
½ to 1 teaspoon cayenne pepper
Chickens:
120 g yogurt
2 small chickens, any giblets removed, split in half lengthwise

1. For the harissa: In a medium microwave-safe bowl, combine the oil, garlic, paprika, coriander, cumin, caraway, salt, and cayenne. Microwave on high for 1 minute, stirring halfway through the cooking time. (You can also heat this on the stovetop until the oil is hot and bubbling. Or, if you must use your air fryer for everything, cook it in the air fryer at 180ºC for 5 to 6 minutes, or until the paste is heated through.) 2. For the chicken: In a small bowl, combine 1 to 2 tablespoons harissa and the yogurt. Whisk until well combined. Place the chicken halves in a resealable plastic bag and pour the marinade over. Seal the bag and massage until all of the pieces are thoroughly coated. Marinate at room temperature for 30 minutes or in the refrigerator for up to 24 hours. 3. Arrange the hen halves in a single layer in the air fryer basket. (If you have a smaller air fryer, you may have to cook this in two batches.) Set the air fryer to 200ºC for 20 minutes. Use a meat thermometer to ensure the chickens have reached an internal temperature of 76ºC.

Thai Curry Meatballs

Prep time: 10 minutes | Cook time: 10 minutes | Serves 4

450 g chicken mince
15 g chopped fresh coriander
1 teaspoon chopped fresh mint
1 tablespoon fresh lime juice
1 tablespoon Thai red, green, or yellow curry paste
1 tablespoon fish sauce
2 garlic cloves, minced
2 teaspoons minced fresh ginger
½ teaspoon kosher salt
½ teaspoon black pepper
¼ teaspoon red pepper flakes

1. Preheat the air fryer to 200ºC. 2. In a large bowl, gently mix the chicken mince, coriander, mint, lime juice, curry paste, fish sauce, garlic, ginger, salt, black pepper, and red pepper flakes until thoroughly combined. 3. Form the mixture into 16 meatballs. Place the meatballs in a single layer in the air fryer basket. Cook for 10 minutes, turning the meatballs halfway through the cooking time. Use a meat thermometer to ensure the meatballs have reached an internal temperature of 76ºC. Serve immediately.

Chicken Patties

Prep time: 15 minutes | Cook time: 12 minutes | Serves 4

450 g chicken thigh mince
110 g shredded Mozzarella cheese
1 teaspoon dried parsley
½ teaspoon garlic powder
¼ teaspoon onion powder
1 large egg
60 g pork rinds, finely ground

1. In a large bowl, mix chicken mince, Mozzarella, parsley, garlic powder, and onion powder. Form into four patties. 2. Place patties in the freezer for 15 to 20 minutes until they begin to firm up. 3. Whisk egg in a medium bowl. Place the ground pork rinds into a large bowl. 4. Dip each chicken patty into the egg and then press into pork rinds to fully coat. Place patties into the air fryer basket. 5. Adjust the temperature to 180ºC and cook for 12 minutes. 6. Patties will be firm and cooked to an internal temperature of 76ºC when done. Serve immediately.

Ginger Turmeric Chicken Thighs

Prep time: 5 minutes | Cook time: 25 minutes | Serves 4

4 (115 g) boneless, skin-on chicken thighs
2 tablespoons coconut oil, melted
½ teaspoon ground turmeric
½ teaspoon salt
½ teaspoon garlic powder
½ teaspoon ground ginger
¼ teaspoon ground black pepper

1. Place chicken thighs in a large bowl and drizzle with coconut oil. Sprinkle with remaining ingredients and toss to coat both sides of thighs. 2. Place thighs skin side up into ungreased air fryer basket. Adjust the temperature to 200ºC and cook for 25 minutes. After 10 minutes, turn thighs. When 5 minutes remain, flip thighs once more. Chicken will be done when skin is golden brown and the internal temperature is at least 76ºC. Serve warm.

Sweet and Spicy Turkey Meatballs

Prep time: 15 minutes | Cook time: 15 minutes | Serves 6

Olive oil
450 g lean turkey mince
60 g whole-wheat panko bread crumbs
1 egg, beaten
1 tablespoon soy sauce
60 ml plus 1 tablespoon hoisin
sauce, divided
2 teaspoons minced garlic
⅛ teaspoon salt
⅛ teaspoon freshly ground black pepper
1 teaspoon Sriracha

1. Spray the air fryer basket lightly with olive oil. 2. In a large bowl, mix together the turkey, panko bread crumbs, egg, soy sauce, 1 tablespoon of hoisin sauce, garlic, salt, and black pepper. 3. Using a tablespoon, form 24 meatballs. 4. In a small bowl, combine the remaining 60 ml of hoisin sauce and Sriracha to make a glaze and set aside. 5. Place the meatballs in the air fryer basket in a single layer. You may need to cook them in batches. 6. Cook at 180ºC for 8 minutes. Brush the meatballs generously with the glaze and cook until cooked through, an additional 4 to 7 minutes.

Jalapeño Popper Hasselback Chicken

Prep time: 10 minutes | Cook time: 19 minutes | Serves 2

Oil, for spraying
2 (230 g) boneless, skinless chicken breasts
60 g cream cheese, softened
55 g bacon bits
20 g chopped pickled jalapeños
40 g shredded Cheddar cheese, divided

1. Line the air fryer basket with parchment and spray lightly with oil. 2. Make multiple cuts across the top of each chicken breast, cutting only halfway through. 3. In a medium bowl, mix together the cream cheese, bacon bits, jalapeños, and Cheddar cheese. Spoon some of the mixture into each cut. 4. Place the chicken in the prepared basket. 5. Cook at 176ºC for 14 minutes. Scatter the remaining cheese on top of the chicken and cook for another 2 to 5 minutes, or until the cheese is melted and the internal temperature reaches 76ºC.

Crispy Dill Chicken Strips

Prep time: 30 minutes | Cook time: 10 minutes | Serves 4

2 whole boneless, skinless chicken breasts (about 450 g each), halved lengthwise
230 ml Italian dressing
110 g finely crushed crisps
1 tablespoon dried dill weed
1 tablespoon garlic powder
1 large egg, beaten
1 to 2 tablespoons oil

1. In a large resealable bag, combine the chicken and Italian dressing. Seal the bag and refrigerate to marinate at least 1 hour. 2. In a shallow dish, stir together the potato chips, dill, and garlic powder. Place the beaten egg in a second shallow dish. 3. Remove the chicken from the marinade. Roll the chicken pieces in the egg and the crisp mixture, coating thoroughly. 4. Preheat the air fryer to 170ºC. Line the air fryer basket with parchment paper. 5. Place the coated chicken on the parchment and spritz with oil. 6. Cook for 5 minutes. Flip the chicken, spritz it with oil, and cook for 5 minutes more until the outsides are crispy and the insides are no longer pink.

Spice-Rubbed Chicken Thighs

Prep time: 10 minutes | Cook time: 25 minutes | Serves 4

4 (115 g) bone-in, skin-on chicken thighs
½ teaspoon salt
½ teaspoon garlic powder
2 teaspoons chili powder
1 teaspoon paprika
1 teaspoon ground cumin
1 small lime, halved

1. Pat chicken thighs dry and sprinkle with salt, garlic powder, chili powder, paprika, and cumin. 2. Squeeze juice from ½ lime over thighs. Place thighs into ungreased air fryer basket. Adjust the temperature to 190ºC and cook for 25 minutes, turning thighs halfway through cooking. Thighs will be crispy and browned with an internal temperature of at least 76ºC when done. 3. Transfer thighs to a large serving plate and drizzle with remaining lime juice. Serve warm.

Crunchy Chicken Tenders

Prep time: 5 minutes | Cook time: 12 minutes | Serves 4

1 egg
60 ml unsweetened almond milk
30 g whole wheat flour
30 g whole wheat bread crumbs
½ teaspoon salt
½ teaspoon black pepper

½ teaspoon dried thyme
½ teaspoon dried sage
½ teaspoon garlic powder
450 g chicken tenderloins
1 lemon, quartered

1. Preheat the air fryer to 184ºC. 2. In a shallow bowl, beat together the egg and almond milk until frothy. 3. In a separate shallow bowl, whisk together the flour, bread crumbs, salt, pepper, thyme, sage, and garlic powder. 4. Dip each chicken tenderloin into the egg mixture, then into the bread crumb mixture, coating the outside with the crumbs. Place the breaded chicken tenderloins into the bottom of the air fryer basket in an even layer, making sure that they don't touch each other. 5. Cook for 6 minutes, then turn and cook for an additional 5 to 6 minutes. Serve with lemon slices.

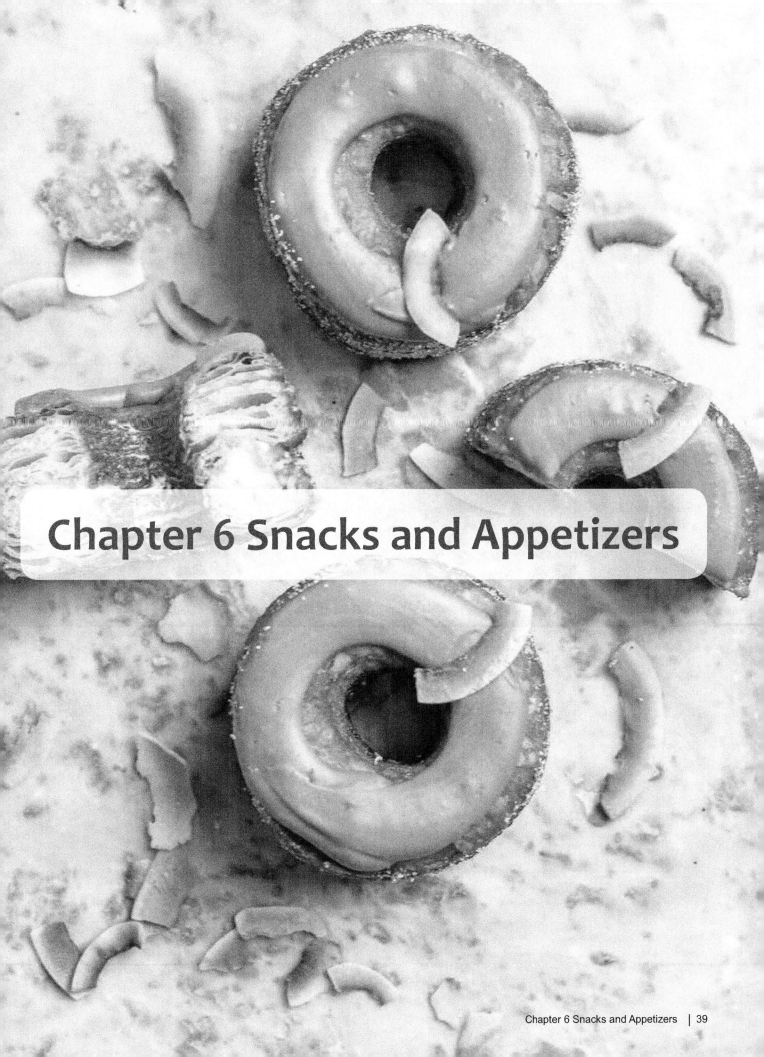

Chapter 6 Snacks and Appetizers

Roasted Grape Dip

Prep time: 10 minutes | Cook time: 8 to 12 minutes | Serves 6

475 ml seedless red grapes, rinsed and patted dry	240 ml low-fat Greek yoghurt
1 tablespoon apple cider vinegar	2 tablespoons semi-skimmed milk
1 tablespoon honey	2 tablespoons minced fresh basil

1. In the air fryer basket, sprinkle the grapes with the cider vinegar and drizzle with the honey. Toss to coat. Cook the grapes at 192°C for 8 to 12 minutes, or until shrivelled but still soft. Remove from the air fryer. 2. In a medium bowl, stir together the yoghurt and milk. 3. Gently blend in the grapes and basil. Serve immediately or cover and chill for 1 to 2 hours.

Five-Ingredient Falafel with Garlic-Yoghurt Sauce

Prep time: 5 minutes | Cook time: 15 minutes | Serves 4

Falafel:	Salt
1 (425 g) can chickpeas, drained and rinsed	Garlic-Yoghurt Sauce:
	240 ml non-fat plain Greek yoghurt
120 ml fresh parsley	
2 garlic cloves, minced	1 garlic clove, minced
½ tablespoon ground cumin	1 tablespoon chopped fresh dill
1 tablespoon wholemeal flour	2 tablespoons lemon juice

Make the Falafel: 1. Preheat the air fryer to 182°C. 2. Put the chickpeas into a food processor. Pulse until mostly chopped, then add the parsley, garlic, and cumin and pulse for another 1 to 2 minutes, or until the ingredients are combined and turning into a dough. 3. Add the flour. Pulse a few more times until combined. The dough will have texture, but the chickpeas should be pulsed into small bits. 4. Using clean hands, roll the dough into 8 balls of equal size, then pat the balls down a bit so they are about ½-thick disks. 5. Spray the basket of the air fryer with olive oil cooking spray, then place the falafel patties in the basket in a single layer, making sure they don't touch each other. 6. Fry in the air fryer for 15 minutes. Make the garlic-yoghurt sauce 7. In a small bowl, combine the yoghurt, garlic, dill, and lemon juice. 8. Once the falafel is done cooking and nicely browned on all sides, remove them from the air fryer and season with salt. 9. Serve hot with a side of dipping sauce.

Bacon-Wrapped Shrimp and Jalapeño

Prep time: 20 minutes | Cook time: 26 minutes | Serves 8

24 large shrimp, peeled and deveined, about 340 g	divided
	12 strips bacon, cut in half
5 tablespoons barbecue sauce,	24 small pickled jalapeño slices

1. Toss together the shrimp and 3 tablespoons of the barbecue sauce. Let stand for 15 minutes. Soak 24 wooden toothpicks in water for 10 minutes. Wrap 1 piece bacon around the shrimp and jalapeño slice, then secure with a toothpick. 2. Preheat the air fryer to 176°C. 3. Working in batches, place half of the shrimp in the air fryer basket, spacing them ½ inch apart. Cook for 10 minutes. Turn shrimp over with tongs and cook for 3 minutes more, or until bacon is golden brown and shrimp are cooked through. 4. Brush with the remaining barbecue sauce and serve.

Parmesan French Fries

Prep time: 10 minutes | Cook time: 15 minutes per batch | Serves 2

2 to 3 large russet or Maris Piper potatoes, peeled and cut into ½-inch sticks	½ teaspoon salt
	Freshly ground black pepper, to taste
2 teaspoons vegetable or rapeseed oil	1 teaspoon fresh chopped parsley
177 ml grated Parmesan cheese	

1. Bring a large saucepan of salted water to a boil on the stovetop while you peel and cut the potatoes. Blanch the potatoes in the boiling salted water for 4 minutes while you preheat the air fryer to 204°C. Strain the potatoes and rinse them with cold water. Dry them well with a clean kitchen towel. 2. Toss the dried potato sticks gently with the oil and place them in the air fryer basket. Cook for 25 minutes, shaking the basket a few times while the fries cook to help them brown evenly. 3. Combine the Parmesan cheese, salt and pepper. With 2 minutes left on the air fryer cooking time, sprinkle the fries with the Parmesan cheese mixture. Toss the fries to coat them evenly with the cheese mixture and continue to cook for the final 2 minutes, until the cheese has melted and just starts to brown. Sprinkle the finished fries with chopped parsley, a little more grated Parmesan cheese if you like, and serve.

Garlic-Parmesan Croutons

Prep time: 3 minutes | Cook time: 12 minutes | Serves 4

Oil, for spraying
1 L cubed French bread
1 tablespoon grated Parmesan cheese
3 tablespoons olive oil
1 tablespoon granulated garlic
½ teaspoon unsalted salt

1. Line the air fryer basket with parchment and spray lightly with oil. 2. In a large bowl, mix together the bread, Parmesan cheese, olive oil, garlic, and salt, tossing with your hands to evenly distribute the seasonings. Transfer the coated bread cubes to the prepared basket. 3. Cook at 176°C for 10 to 12 minutes, stirring once after 5 minutes, or until crisp and golden brown.

Courgette Fries with Roasted Garlic Aioli

Prep time: 20 minutes | Cook time: 12 minutes | Serves 4

1 tablespoon vegetable oil
½ head green or savoy cabbage, finely shredded
Roasted Garlic Aioli:
1 teaspoon roasted garlic
120 ml mayonnaise
2 tablespoons olive oil
Juice of ½ lemon
Salt and pepper, to taste
Courgette Fries:
120 ml flour
2 eggs, beaten
240 ml seasoned breadcrumbs
Salt and pepper, to taste
1 large courgette, cut into ½-inch sticks
Olive oil

1. Make the aioli: Combine the roasted garlic, mayonnaise, olive oil and lemon juice in a bowl and whisk well. Season the aioli with salt and pepper to taste. 2. Prepare the courgette fries. Create a dredging station with three shallow dishes. Place the flour in the first shallow dish and season well with salt and freshly ground black pepper. Put the beaten eggs in the second shallow dish. In the third shallow dish, combine the breadcrumbs, salt and pepper. Dredge the courgette sticks, coating with flour first, then dipping them into the eggs to coat, and finally tossing in breadcrumbs. Shake the dish with the breadcrumbs and pat the crumbs onto the courgette sticks gently with your hands, so they stick evenly. 3. Place the courgette fries on a flat surface and let them sit at least 10 minutes before air frying to let them dry out a little. Preheat the air fryer to 204°C. 4. Spray the courgette sticks with olive oil and place them into the air fryer basket. You can cook the courgette in two layers, placing the second layer in the opposite direction to the first. Cook for 12 minutes turning and rotating the fries halfway through the cooking time. Spray with additional oil when you turn them over. 5. Serve courgette fries warm with the roasted garlic aioli.

Shishito Peppers with Herb Dressing

Prep time: 10 minutes | Cook time: 6 minutes | Serves 2 to 4

170 g shishito or Padron peppers
1 tablespoon vegetable oil
Rock salt and freshly ground black pepper, to taste
120 ml mayonnaise
2 tablespoons finely chopped fresh basil leaves
2 tablespoons finely chopped
fresh flat-leaf parsley
1 tablespoon finely chopped fresh tarragon
1 tablespoon finely chopped fresh chives
Finely grated zest of ½ lemon
1 tablespoon fresh lemon juice
Flaky sea salt, for serving

1. Preheat the air fryer to 204°C. 2. In a bowl, toss together the shishitos and oil to evenly coat and season with rock salt and black pepper. Transfer to the air fryer and cook for 6 minutes, shaking the basket halfway through, or until the shishitos are blistered and lightly charred. 3. Meanwhile, in a small bowl, whisk together the mayonnaise, basil, parsley, tarragon, chives, lemon zest, and lemon juice. 4. Pile the peppers on a plate, sprinkle with flaky sea salt, and serve hot with the dressing.

Hush Puppies

Prep time: 45 minutes | Cook time: 10 minutes | Serves 12

240 ml self-raising yellow cornmeal
120 ml plain flour
1 teaspoon sugar
1 teaspoon salt
1 teaspoon freshly ground black pepper
1 large egg
80 ml canned creamed corn
240 ml minced onion
2 teaspoons minced jalapeño pepper
2 tablespoons olive oil, divided

1. Thoroughly combine the cornmeal, flour, sugar, salt, and pepper in a large bowl. 2. Whisk together the egg and corn in a small bowl. Pour the egg mixture into the bowl of cornmeal mixture and stir to combine. Stir in the minced onion and jalapeño. Cover the bowl with plastic wrap and place in the refrigerator for 30 minutes. 3. Preheat the air fryer to 192°C. Line the air fryer basket with parchment paper and lightly brush it with 1 tablespoon of olive oil. 4. Scoop out the cornmeal mixture and form into 24 balls, about 1 inch. 5. Arrange the balls in the parchment paper-lined basket, leaving space between each ball. 6. Cook in batches for 5 minutes. Shake the basket and brush the balls with the remaining 1 tablespoon of olive oil. Continue cooking for 5 minutes until golden brown. 7. Remove the balls (hush puppies) from the basket and serve on a plate.

Cinnamon-Apple Crisps

Prep time: 10 minutes | Cook time: 32 minutes | Serves 4

Oil, for spraying
2 Red Delicious or Honeycrisp apples

¼ teaspoon ground cinnamon, divided

1. Line the air fryer basket with parchment and spray lightly with oil. 2. Trim the uneven ends off the apples. Using a mandoline slicer on the thinnest setting or a sharp knife, cut the apples into very thin slices. Discard the cores. 3. Place half of the apple slices in a single layer in the prepared basket and sprinkle with half of the cinnamon. 4. Place a metal air fryer trivet on top of the apples to keep them from flying around while they are cooking. 5. Cook at 148°C for 16 minutes, flipping every 5 minutes to ensure even cooking. Repeat with the remaining apple slices and cinnamon. 6. Let cool to room temperature before serving. The crisps will firm up as they cool.

Goat Cheese and Garlic Crostini

Prep time: 3 minutes | Cook time: 5 minutes | Serves 4

1 wholemeal baguette
60 ml olive oil
2 garlic cloves, minced

113 g goat cheese
2 tablespoons fresh basil, minced

1. Preheat the air fryer to 192°C. 2. Cut the baguette into ½-inch-thick slices. 3. In a small bowl, mix together the olive oil and garlic, then brush it over one side of each slice of bread. 4. Place the olive-oil-coated bread in a single layer in the air fryer basket and cook for 5 minutes. 5. Meanwhile, in a small bowl, mix together the goat cheese and basil. 6. Remove the toast from the air fryer, then spread a thin layer of the goat cheese mixture over the top of each piece and serve.

Garlic Edamame

Prep time: 5 minutes | Cook time: 10 minutes | Serves 4

Olive oil
1 (454 g) bag frozen edamame in pods
½ teaspoon salt
½ teaspoon garlic salt

¼ teaspoon freshly ground black pepper
½ teaspoon red pepper flakes (optional)

1. Spray the air fryer basket lightly with olive oil. 2. In a medium bowl, add the frozen edamame and lightly spray with olive oil. Toss to coat. 3. In a small bowl, mix together the salt, garlic salt, black pepper, and red pepper flakes (if using). Add the mixture to the edamame and toss until evenly coated. 4. Place half the edamame in the air fryer basket. Do not overfill the basket. 5. Cook at 192°C for 5 minutes. Shake the basket and cook until the edamame is starting to brown and get crispy, 3 to 5 more minutes. 6. Repeat with the remaining edamame and serve immediately.

Red Pepper Tapenade

Prep time: 5 minutes | Cook time: 5 minutes | Serves 4

1 large red pepper
2 tablespoons plus 1 teaspoon olive oil, divided
120 ml Kalamata olives, pitted

and roughly chopped
1 garlic clove, minced
½ teaspoon dried oregano
1 tablespoon lemon juice

1. Preheat the air fryer to 192°C. 2. Brush the outside of a whole red pepper with 1 teaspoon olive oil and place it inside the air fryer basket. Cook for 5 minutes. 3. Meanwhile, in a medium bowl, combine the remaining 2 tablespoons of olive oil with the olives, garlic, oregano, and lemon juice. 4. Remove the red pepper from the air fryer, then gently slice off the stem and remove the seeds. Roughly chop the roasted pepper into small pieces. 5. Add the red pepper to the olive mixture and stir all together until combined. 6. Serve with pitta chips, crackers, or crusty bread.

Cheesy Courgette Tots

Prep time: 15 minutes | Cook time: 6 minutes | Serves 8

2 medium courgette (about 340 g), shredded
1 large egg, whisked
120 ml grated pecorino Romano cheese

120 ml panko breadcrumbs
¼ teaspoon black pepper
1 clove garlic, minced
Cooking spray

1. Using your hands, squeeze out as much liquid from the courgette as possible. In a large bowl, mix the courgette with the remaining ingredients except the oil until well incorporated. 2. Make the courgette tots: Use a spoon or cookie scoop to place tablespoonfuls of the courgette mixture onto a lightly floured cutting board and form into 1-inch logs. 3. Preheat air fryer to 192°C. Spritz the air fryer basket with cooking spray. 4. Place the tots in the basket. You may need to cook in batches to avoid overcrowding. 5. Cook for 6 minutes until golden brown. 6. Remove from the basket to a serving plate and repeat with the remaining courgette tots. 7. Serve immediately.

Skinny Fries

Prep time: 10 minutes | Cook time: 15 minutes per batch | Serves 2

2 to 3 russet or Maris Piper potatoes, peeled and cut into ¼-inch sticks

2 to 3 teaspoons olive or vegetable oil
Salt, to taste

1. Cut the potatoes into ¼-inch strips. (A mandolin with a julienne blade is really helpful here.) Rinse the potatoes with cold water several times and let them soak in cold water for at least 10 minutes or as long as overnight. 2. Preheat the air fryer to 192°C. 3. Drain and dry the potato sticks really well, using a clean kitchen towel. Toss the fries with the oil in a bowl and then cook the fries in two batches at 192°C for 15 minutes, shaking the basket a couple of times while they cook. 4. Add the first batch of French fries back into the air fryer basket with the finishing batch and let everything warm through for a few minutes. As soon as the fries are done, season them with salt and transfer to a plate or basket. Serve them warm with ketchup or your favourite dip.

Chilli-Brined Fried Calamari

Prep time: 20 minutes | Cook time: 8 minutes | Serves 2

1 (227 g) jar sweet or hot pickled cherry peppers
227 g calamari bodies and tentacles, bodies cut into ½-inch-wide rings
1 lemon
475 ml plain flour
Rock salt and freshly ground

black pepper, to taste
3 large eggs, lightly beaten
Cooking spray
120 ml mayonnaise
1 teaspoon finely chopped rosemary
1 garlic clove, minced

1. Drain the pickled pepper brine into a large bowl and tear the peppers into bite-size strips. Add the pepper strips and calamari to the brine and let stand in the refrigerator for 20 minutes or up to 2 hours. 2. Grate the lemon zest into a large bowl then whisk in the flour and season with salt and pepper. Dip the calamari and pepper strips in the egg, then toss them in the flour mixture until fully coated. Spray the calamari and peppers liberally with cooking spray, then transfer half to the air fryer. Cook at 204°C, shaking the basket halfway into cooking, until the calamari is cooked through and golden brown, about 8 minutes. Transfer to a plate and repeat with the remaining pieces. 3. In a small bowl, whisk together the mayonnaise, rosemary, and garlic. Squeeze half the zested lemon to get 1 tablespoon of juice and stir it into the sauce. Season with salt and pepper. Cut the remaining zested lemon half into 4 small wedges and serve alongside the calamari, peppers, and sauce.

Crispy Breaded Beef Cubes

Prep time: 10 minutes | Cook time: 12 to 16 minutes | Serves 4

450 g sirloin tip, cut into 1-inch cubes
240 ml cheese pasta sauce

355 ml soft breadcrumbs
2 tablespoons olive oil
½ teaspoon dried marjoram

1. Preheat the air fryer to 182°C. 2. In a medium bowl, toss the beef with the pasta sauce to coat. 3. In a shallow bowl, combine the breadcrumbs, oil, and marjoram, and mix well. Drop the beef cubes, one at a time, into the bread crumb mixture to coat thoroughly. 4. Cook the beef in two batches for 6 to 8 minutes, shaking the basket once during cooking time, until the beef is at least 63°C and the outside is crisp and brown. 5. Serve hot.

Veggie Salmon Nachos

Prep time: 10 minutes | Cook time: 9 to 12 minutes | Serves 6

57 g baked no-salt corn tortilla chips
1 (142 g) baked salmon fillet, flaked
120 ml canned low-salt black beans, rinsed and drained

1 red pepper, chopped
120 ml grated carrot
1 jalapeño pepper, minced
80 ml shredded low-salt low-fat Swiss cheese
1 tomato, chopped

1. Preheat the air fryer to 182°C. 2. In a baking pan, layer the tortilla chips. Top with the salmon, black beans, red pepper, carrot, jalapeño, and Swiss cheese. 3. Cook in the air fryer for 9 to 12 minutes, or until the cheese is melted and starts to brown. 4. Top with the tomato and serve.

Spicy Chicken Bites

Prep time: 10 minutes | Cook time: 10 to 12 minutes | Makes 30 bites

227 g boneless and skinless chicken thighs, cut into 30 pieces

¼ teaspoon rock salt
2 tablespoons hot sauce
Cooking spray

1. Preheat the air fryer to 200°C. 2. Spray the air fryer basket with cooking spray and season the chicken bites with the rock salt, then place in the basket and cook for 10 to 12 minutes or until crispy. 3. While the chicken bites cook, pour the hot sauce into a large bowl. 4. Remove the bites and add to the sauce bowl, tossing to coat. Serve warm.

Beef and Mango Skewers

Prep time: 10 minutes | Cook time: 4 to 7 minutes | Serves 4

340 g beef sirloin tip, cut into 1-inch cubes
2 tablespoons balsamic vinegar
1 tablespoon olive oil
1 tablespoon honey
½ teaspoon dried marjoram
Pinch of salt
Freshly ground black pepper, to taste
1 mango

1. Preheat the air fryer to 200ºC. 2. Put the beef cubes in a medium bowl and add the balsamic vinegar, olive oil, honey, marjoram, salt, and pepper. Mix well, then massage the marinade into the beef with your hands. Set aside. 3. To prepare the mango, stand it on end and cut the skin off, using a sharp knife. Then carefully cut around the oval pit to remove the flesh. Cut the mango into 1-inch cubes. 4. Thread metal skewers alternating with three beef cubes and two mango cubes. 5. Cook the skewers in the air fryer basket for 4 to 7 minutes, or until the beef is browned and at least 63ºC. 6. Serve hot.

Classic Spring Rolls

Prep time: 10 minutes | Cook time: 9 minutes | Makes 16 spring rolls

4 teaspoons toasted sesame oil
6 medium garlic cloves, minced or pressed
1 tablespoon grated peeled fresh ginger
475 ml thinly sliced shiitake mushrooms
1 L chopped green cabbage
240 ml grated carrot
½ teaspoon sea salt
16 rice paper wrappers
Cooking oil spray (sunflower, safflower, or refined coconut)
Gluten-free sweet and sour sauce or Thai sweet chilli sauce, for serving (optional)

1. Place a wok or sauté pan over medium heat until hot. 2. Add the sesame oil, garlic, ginger, mushrooms, cabbage, carrot, and salt. Cook for 3 to 4 minutes, stirring often, until the cabbage is lightly wilted. Remove the pan from the heat. 3. Gently run a rice paper under water. Lay it on a flat non-absorbent surface. Place about 60 ml of the cabbage filling in the middle. Once the wrapper is soft enough to roll, fold the bottom up over the filling, fold in the sides, and roll the wrapper all the way up. (Basically, make a tiny burrito.) 4. Repeat step 3 to make the remaining spring rolls until you have the number of spring rolls you want to cook right now (and the amount that will fit in the air fryer basket in a single layer without them touching each other). Refrigerate any leftover filling in an airtight container for about 1 week. 5. Insert the crisper plate into the basket and the basket into the unit. Preheat the unit by selecting AIR FRY, setting the temperature to 200ºC, and setting the time to 3 minutes. Select START/STOP to begin. 6. Once the unit is preheated, spray the crisper plate and the basket with cooking oil.

Place the spring rolls into the basket, leaving a little room between them so they don't stick to each other. Spray the top of each spring roll with cooking oil. 7. Select AIR FRY, set the temperature to 200ºC, and set the time to 9 minutes. Select START/STOP to begin. 8. When the cooking is complete, the egg rolls should be crisp-ish and lightly browned. Serve immediately, plain or with a sauce of choice.

Homemade Sweet Potato Chips

Prep time: 5 minutes | Cook time: 15 minutes | Serves 2

1 large sweet potato, sliced thin
⅛ teaspoon salt
2 tablespoons olive oil

1. Preheat the air fryer to 192ºC. 2. In a small bowl, toss the sweet potatoes, salt, and olive oil together until the potatoes are well coated. 3. Put the sweet potato slices into the air fryer and spread them out in a single layer. 4. Fry for 10 minutes. Stir, then cook for 3 to 5 minutes more, or until the chips reach the preferred level of crispiness.

Lemon Shrimp with Garlic Olive Oil

Prep time: 5 minutes | Cook time: 6 minutes | Serves 4

454 g medium shrimp, cleaned and deveined
60 ml plus 2 tablespoons olive oil, divided
Juice of ½ lemon
3 garlic cloves, minced and divided
½ teaspoon salt
¼ teaspoon red pepper flakes
Lemon wedges, for serving (optional)
Marinara sauce, for dipping (optional)

1. Preheat the air fryer to 192ºC. 2. In a large bowl, combine the shrimp with 2 tablespoons of the olive oil, as well as the lemon juice, ⅓ of the minced garlic, salt, and red pepper flakes. Toss to coat the shrimp well. 3. In a small ramekin, combine the remaining 60 ml of olive oil and the remaining minced garlic. 4. Tear off a 12-by-12-inch sheet of aluminium foil. Pour the shrimp into the centre of the foil, then fold the sides up and crimp the edges so that it forms an aluminium foil bowl that is open on top. Place this packet into the air fryer basket. 5. Cook the shrimp for 4 minutes, then open the air fryer and place the ramekin with oil and garlic in the basket beside the shrimp packet. Cook for 2 more minutes. 6. Transfer the shrimp on a serving plate or platter with the ramekin of garlic olive oil on the side for dipping. You may also serve with lemon wedges and marinara sauce, if desired.

Turkey Burger Sliders

Prep time: 10 minutes | Cook time: 5 to 7 minutes | Makes 8 sliders

450 g minced turkey	120 ml slivered red onions
¼ teaspoon curry powder	120 ml slivered green or red
1 teaspoon Hoisin sauce	pepper
½ teaspoon salt	120 ml fresh chopped pineapple
8 slider rolls	Light soft white cheese

1. Combine turkey, curry powder, Hoisin sauce, and salt and mix together well. 2. Shape turkey mixture into 8 small patties. 3. Place patties in air fryer basket and cook at 182°C for 5 to 7 minutes, until patties are well done, and juices run clear. 4. Place each patty on the bottom half of a slider roll and top with onions, peppers, and pineapple. Spread the remaining bun halves with soft white cheese to taste, place on top, and serve.

Jalapeño Poppers

Prep time: 10 minutes | Cook time: 20 minutes | Serves 4

Oil, for spraying	parsley
227 g soft white cheese	½ teaspoon granulated garlic
177 ml gluten-free breadcrumbs, divided	½ teaspoon salt
2 tablespoons chopped fresh	10 jalapeño peppers, halved and seeded

1. Line the air fryer basket with parchment and spray lightly with oil. 2. In a medium bowl, mix together the soft white cheese, half of the breadcrumbs, the parsley, garlic, and salt. 3. Spoon the mixture into the jalapeño halves. Gently press the stuffed jalapeños in the remaining breadcrumbs. 4. Place the stuffed jalapeños in the prepared basket. 5. Cook at 188°C for 20 minutes, or until the cheese is melted and the breadcrumbs are crisp and golden brown.

Tortellini with Spicy Dipping Sauce

Prep time: 5 minutes | Cook time: 20 minutes | Serves 4

177 ml mayonnaise	½ teaspoon dried oregano
2 tablespoons mustard	355 ml breadcrumbs
1 egg	2 tablespoons olive oil
120 ml flour	475 ml frozen cheese tortellini

1. Preheat the air fryer to 192°C. 2. In a small bowl, combine the mayonnaise and mustard and mix well. Set aside. 3. In a shallow bowl, beat the egg. In a separate bowl, combine the flour and oregano. In another bowl, combine the breadcrumbs and olive

oil, and mix well. 4. Drop the tortellini, a few at a time, into the egg, then into the flour, then into the egg again, and then into the breadcrumbs to coat. Put into the air fryer basket, cooking in batches. 5. Cook for about 10 minutes, shaking halfway through the cooking time, or until the tortellini are crisp and golden brown on the outside. Serve with the mayonnaise mixture.

Stuffed Figs with Goat Cheese and Honey

Prep time: 5 minutes | Cook time: 10 minutes | Serves 4

8 fresh figs	1 tablespoon honey, plus more
57 g goat cheese	for serving
¼ teaspoon ground cinnamon	1 tablespoon olive oil

1. Preheat the air fryer to 182°C. Line an 8-by-8-inch baking dish with parchment paper that comes up the side so you can lift it out after cooking. 2. In a large bowl, mix together all of the ingredients until well combined. 3. Press the oat mixture into the pan in an even layer. 4. Place the pan into the air fryer basket and cook for 15 minutes. 5. Remove the pan from the air fryer and lift the granola cake out of the pan using the edges of the parchment paper. 6. Allow to cool for 5 minutes before slicing into 6 equal bars. 7. Serve immediately or wrap in plastic wrap and store at room temperature for up to 1 week.

Crispy Filo Artichoke Triangles

Prep time: 15 minutes | Cook time: 9 to 12 minutes | Makes 18 triangles

60 ml Ricotta cheese	cheese
1 egg white	½ teaspoon dried thyme
80 ml minced and drained artichoke hearts	6 sheets frozen filo pastry, thawed
3 tablespoons grated Mozzarella	2 tablespoons melted butter

1. Preheat the air fryer to 204°C. 2. In a small bowl, combine the Ricotta cheese, egg white, artichoke hearts, Mozzarella cheese, and thyme, and mix well. 3. Cover the filo pastry with a damp kitchen towel while you work so it doesn't dry out. Using one sheet at a time, place on the work surface and cut into thirds lengthwise. 4. Put about 1½ teaspoons of the filling on each strip at the base. Fold the bottom right-hand tip of phyllo over the filling to meet the other side in a triangle, then continue folding in a triangle. Brush each triangle with butter to seal the edges. Repeat with the remaining phyllo dough and filling. 5. Place the triangles in the air fryer basket. Bake, 6 at a time, for about 3 to 4 minutes, or until the filo is golden brown and crisp. 6. Serve hot.

Bruschetta with Basil Pesto

Prep time: 10 minutes | Cook time: 5 to 11 minutes | Serves 4

8 slices French bread, ½ inch thick

2 tablespoons softened butter

240 ml shredded Mozzarella cheese

120 ml basil pesto

240 ml chopped grape tomatoes

2 spring onions, thinly sliced

1. Preheat the air fryer to 176°C. 2. Spread the bread with the butter and place butter-side up in the air fryer basket. Cook for 3 to 5 minutes, or until the bread is light golden brown. 3. Remove the bread from the basket and top each piece with some of the cheese. Return to the basket in 2 batches and cook for 1 to 3 minutes, or until the cheese melts. 4. Meanwhile, combine the pesto, tomatoes, and spring onions in a small bowl. 5. When the cheese has melted, remove the bread from the air fryer and place on a serving plate. Top each slice with some of the pesto mixture and serve.

Lemony Pear Chips

Prep time: 15 minutes | Cook time: 9 to 13 minutes | Serves 4

2 firm Bosc or Anjou pears, cut crosswise into ⅛-inch-thick slices

1 tablespoon freshly squeezed lemon juice

½ teaspoon ground cinnamon

⅛ teaspoon ground cardamom

1. Preheat the air fryer to 192°C. 2. Separate the smaller stem-end pear rounds from the larger rounds with seeds. Remove the core and seeds from the larger slices. Sprinkle all slices with lemon juice, cinnamon, and cardamom. 3. Put the smaller chips into the air fryer basket. Cook for 3 to 5 minutes, or until light golden brown, shaking the basket once during cooking. Remove from the air fryer. 4. Repeat with the larger slices, air frying for 6 to 8 minutes, or until light golden brown, shaking the basket once during cooking. 5. Remove the chips from the air fryer. Cool and serve or store in an airtight container at room temperature up for to 2 days.

Kale Chips with Sesame

Prep time: 15 minutes | Cook time: 8 minutes | Serves 5

2 L deribbed kale leaves, torn into 2-inch pieces

1½ tablespoons olive oil

¾ teaspoon chilli powder

¼ teaspoon garlic powder

½ teaspoon paprika

2 teaspoons sesame seeds

1. Preheat air fryer to 176°C. 2. In a large bowl, toss the kale with the olive oil, chilli powder, garlic powder, paprika, and sesame seeds until well coated. 3. Put the kale in the air fryer basket and cook for 8 minutes, flipping the kale twice during cooking, or until the kale is crispy. 4. Serve warm.

Chapter 7 Fish and Seafood

Chapter 7 Fish and Seafood

Savory Prawns

Prep time: 5 minutes | Cook time: 8 to 10 minutes | Serves 4

455 g fresh large prawns, peeled and deveined
1 tablespoon avocado oil
2 teaspoons minced garlic, divided
½ teaspoon red pepper flakes

Sea salt and freshly ground black pepper, to taste
2 tablespoons unsalted butter, melted
2 tablespoons chopped fresh parsley

1. Place the prawns in a large bowl and toss with the avocado oil, 1 teaspoon of minced garlic, and red pepper flakes. Season with salt and pepper. 2. Set the air fryer to 176°C. Arrange the prawns in a single layer in the air fryer basket, working in batches if necessary. Cook for 6 minutes. Flip the prawns and cook for 2 to 4 minutes more, until the internal temperature of the prawns reaches 50°C. (The time it takes to cook will depend on the size of the prawns.) 3. While the prawns are cooking, melt the butter in a small saucepan over medium heat and stir in the remaining 1 teaspoon of garlic. 4. Transfer the cooked prawns to a large bowl, add the garlic butter, and toss well. Top with the parsley and serve warm.

Crunchy Fish Sticks

Prep time: 30 minutes | Cook time: 9 minutes | Serves 4

455 g cod fillets
170 g finely ground blanched almond flour
2 teaspoons Old Bay seasoning
½ teaspoon paprika
Sea salt and freshly ground

black pepper, to taste
60 ml mayonnaise
1 large egg, beaten
Avocado oil spray
Tartar sauce, for serving

1. Cut the fish into ¾-inch-wide strips. 2. In a shallow bowl, stir together the almond flour, Old Bay seasoning, paprika, and salt and pepper to taste. In another shallow bowl, whisk together the mayonnaise and egg. 3. Dip the cod strips in the egg mixture, then the almond flour, gently pressing with your fingers to help adhere to the coating. 4. Place the coated fish on a baking paper -lined baking sheet and freeze for 30 minutes. 5. Spray the air fryer basket with oil. Set the air fryer to 204°C. Place the fish in the basket in a single layer, and spray each piece with oil. 6. Cook for 5 minutes. Flip and spray with more oil. Cook for 4 minutes more, until the internal temperature reaches 60°C. Serve with the tartar sauce.

Smoky Prawns and Chorizo Tapas

Prep time: 15 minutes | Cook time: 10 minutes | Serves 2 to 4

110 g Spanish (cured) chorizo, halved horizontally and sliced crosswise
230 g raw medium prawns, peeled and deveined
1 tablespoon extra-virgin olive oil
1 small shallot, halved and thinly sliced
1 garlic clove, minced

1 tablespoon finely chopped fresh oregano
½ teaspoon smoked Spanish paprika
¼ teaspoon kosher or coarse sea salt
¼ teaspoon black pepper
3 tablespoons fresh orange juice
1 tablespoon minced fresh parsley

1. Place the chorizo in a baking pan. Set the pan in the air fryer basket. Set the air fryer to 192°C for 5 minutes, or until the chorizo has started to brown and render its fat. 2. Meanwhile, in a large bowl, combine the prawns, olive oil, shallot, garlic, oregano, paprika, salt, and pepper. Toss until the prawns are well coated. 3. Transfer the prawns to the pan with the chorizo. Stir to combine. Place the pan in the air fryer basket. Cook for 10 minutes, stirring halfway through the cooking time. 4. Transfer the prawns and chorizo to a serving dish. Drizzle with the orange juice and toss to combine. Sprinkle with the parsley.

Crab Cakes with Bell Peppers

Prep time: 5 minutes | Cook time: 10 minutes | Serves 4

230 g jumbo lump crab meat
1 egg, beaten
Juice of ½ lemon
50 g bread crumbs
35 g diced green bell pepper

35 g diced red bell pepper
60 g mayonnaise
1 tablespoon Old Bay seasoning
1 teaspoon plain flour
Cooking spray

1. Preheat the air fryer to 190°C. 2. Make the crab cakes: Place all the ingredients except the flour and oil in a large bowl and stir until well incorporated. 3. Divide the crab mixture into four equal portions and shape each portion into a patty with your hands. Top each patty with a sprinkle of ¼ teaspoon of flour. 4. Arrange the crab cakes in the air fryer basket and spritz them with cooking spray. 5. Cook for 10 minutes, flipping the crab cakes halfway through, or until they are cooked through. 6. Divide the crab cakes among four plates and serve.

Fish Cakes

Prep time: 30 minutes | Cook time: 10 to 12 minutes | Serves 4

1 large russet potato, mashed
340 g cod or other white fish
Salt and pepper, to taste
Olive or vegetable oil for misting or cooking spray
1 large egg
50 g potato starch
60 g panko breadcrumbs
1 tablespoon fresh chopped chives
2 tablespoons minced onion

1. Peel potatoes, cut into cubes, and cook on stovetop till soft. 2. Salt and pepper raw fish to taste. Mist with oil or cooking spray, and cook at 182°C for 6 to 8 minutes, until fish flakes easily. If fish is crowded, rearrange halfway through cooking to ensure all pieces cook evenly. 3. Transfer fish to a plate and break apart to cool. 4. Beat egg in a shallow dish. 5. Place potato starch in another shallow dish, and panko crumbs in a third dish. 6. When potatoes are done, drain in colander and rinse with cold water. 7. In a large bowl, mash the potatoes and stir in the chives and onion. Add salt and pepper to taste, then stir in the fish. 8. If needed, stir in a tablespoon of the beaten egg to help bind the mixture. 9. Shape into 8 small, fat patties. Dust lightly with potato starch, dip in egg, and roll in panko crumbs. Spray both sides with oil or cooking spray. 10. Cook for 10 to 12 minutes, until golden brown and crispy.

Cod Tacos with Mango Salsa

Prep time: 15 minutes | Cook time: 17 minutes | Serves 4

1 mango, peeled and diced
1 small jalapeño pepper, diced
½ red bell pepper, diced
½ red onion, minced
Pinch chopped fresh cilantro
Juice of ½ lime
¼ teaspoon salt
¼ teaspoon ground black pepper
120 ml Mexican beer
1 egg
75 g cornflour
90 g plain flour
½ teaspoon ground cumin
¼ teaspoon chilli powder
455 g cod, cut into 4 pieces
Olive oil spray
4 corn tortillas, or flour tortillas, at room temperature

1. In a small bowl, stir together the mango, jalapeño, red bell pepper, red onion, cilantro, lime juice, salt, and pepper. Set aside. 2. In a medium bowl, whisk the beer and egg. 3. In another medium bowl, stir together the cornflour, flour, cumin, and chilli powder. 4. Insert the crisper plate into the basket and the basket into the unit. Preheat the unit to 192°C. 5. Dip the fish pieces into the egg mixture and in the flour mixture to coat completely. 6. Once the unit is preheated, place a baking paper liner into the basket. Place the fish on the liner in a single layer. 7. Cook for about 9 minutes, spray the fish with olive oil. Reinsert the basket to resume cooking. 8. When the cooking is complete, the fish should be golden and crispy. Place the pieces in the tortillas, top with the mango salsa, and serve.

Ahi Tuna Steaks

Prep time: 5 minutes | Cook time: 14 minutes | Serves 2

2 ahi tuna steaks, 170g each
2 tablespoons olive oil
3 tablespoons everything bagel seasoning

1. Drizzle both sides of each steak with olive oil. Place seasoning on a medium plate and press each side of tuna steaks into seasoning to form a thick layer. 2. Place steaks into ungreased air fryer basket. Adjust the temperature to204°C and cook for 14 minutes, turning steaks halfway through cooking. Steaks will be done when internal temperature is at least 64°C for well-done. Serve warm.

Tuna with Herbs

Prep time: 20 minutes | Cook time: 17 minutes | Serves 4

1 tablespoon butter, melted
1 medium-sized leek, thinly sliced
1 tablespoon chicken stock
1 tablespoon dry white wine
455 g tuna
½ teaspoon red pepper flakes, crushed
Sea salt and ground black pepper, to taste
½ teaspoon dried rosemary
½ teaspoon dried basil
½ teaspoon dried thyme
2 small ripe tomatoes, puréed
120 g Parmesan cheese, grated

1. Melt ½ tablespoon of butter in a sauté pan over medium-high heat. Now, cook the leek and garlic until tender and aromatic. Add the stock and wine to deglaze the pan. 2. Preheat the air fryer to 188°C. 3. Grease a casserole dish with the remaining ½ tablespoon of melted butter. Place the fish in the casserole dish. Add the seasonings. Top with the sautéed leek mixture. Add the tomato purée. Cook for 10 minutes in the preheated air fryer. Top with grated Parmesan cheese; cook an additional 7 minutes until the crumbs are golden. Bon appétit!

Prawn Bake

Prep time: 15 minutes | Cook time: 5 minutes | Serves 4

400 g prawns, peeled and deveined
1 egg, beaten
120 ml coconut milk
120 g Cheddar cheese, shredded
½ teaspoon coconut oil
1 teaspoon ground coriander

1. In the mixing bowl, mix prawns with egg, coconut milk, Cheddar cheese, coconut oil, and ground coriander. 2. Then put the mixture in the baking ramekins and put in the air fryer. 3. Cook the prawns at 204°C for 5 minutes.

Black Cod with Grapes and Kale

Prep time: 10 minutes | Cook time: 15 minutes | Serves 2

2 fillets of black cod, 200 g each
Salt and freshly ground black pepper, to taste
Olive oil
150 g grapes, halved
1 small bulb fennel, sliced ¼-inch thick

65 g pecans
200 g shredded kale
2 teaspoons white balsamic vinegar or white wine vinegar
2 tablespoons extra-virgin olive oil

1. Preheat the air fryer to 204°C. 2. Season the cod fillets with salt and pepper and drizzle, brush or spray a little olive oil on top. Place the fish, presentation side up (skin side down), into the air fryer basket. Cook for 10 minutes. 3. When the fish has finished cooking, remove the fillets to a side plate and loosely tent with foil to rest. 4. Toss the grapes, fennel and pecans in a bowl with a drizzle of olive oil and season with salt and pepper. Add the grapes, fennel and pecans to the air fryer basket and cook for 5 minutes, shaking the basket once during the cooking time. 5. Transfer the grapes, fennel and pecans to a bowl with the kale. Dress the kale with the balsamic vinegar and olive oil, season to taste with salt and pepper and serve alongside the cooked fish.

Scallops with Asparagus and Peas

Prep time: 10 minutes | Cook time: 7 to 10 minutes | Serves 4

Cooking oil spray
455 g asparagus, ends trimmed, cut into 2-inch pieces
100 g sugar snap peas
455 g sea scallops
1 tablespoon freshly squeezed

lemon juice
2 teaspoons extra-virgin olive oil
½ teaspoon dried thyme
Salt and freshly ground black pepper, to taste

1. Insert the crisper plate into the basket and the basket into the unit. Preheat the unit to 204°C. 2. Once the unit is preheated, spray the crisper plate with cooking oil. Place the asparagus and sugar snap peas into the basket. 3. Cook for 10 minutes. 4. Meanwhile, check the scallops for a small muscle attached to the side. Pull it off and discard. In a medium bowl, toss together the scallops, lemon juice, olive oil, and thyme. Season with salt and pepper. 5. After 3 minutes, the vegetables should be just starting to get tender. Place the scallops on top of the vegetables. Reinsert the basket to resume cooking. After 3 minutes more, remove the basket and shake it. Again reinsert the basket to resume cooking. 6. When the cooking is complete, the scallops should be firm when tested with your finger and opaque in the center, and the vegetables tender. Serve immediately.

Fried Prawns

Prep time: 15 minutes | Cook time: 5 minutes | Serves 4

70 g self-raising flour
1 teaspoon paprika
1 teaspoon salt
½ teaspoon freshly ground black pepper
1 large egg, beaten

120 g finely crushed panko bread crumbs
20 frozen large prawns (about 900 g), peeled and deveined
Cooking spray

1. In a shallow bowl, whisk the flour, paprika, salt, and pepper until blended. Add the beaten egg to a second shallow bowl and the bread crumbs to a third. 2. One at a time, dip the prawns into the flour, the egg, and the bread crumbs, coating thoroughly. 3. Preheat the air fryer to 204°C. Line the air fryer basket with baking paper. 4. Place the prawns on the baking paper and spritz with oil. 5. Cook for 2 minutes. Shake the basket, spritz the prawns with oil, and cook for 3 minutes more until lightly browned and crispy. Serve hot.

Nutty Prawns with Amaretto Glaze

Prep time: 30 minutes | Cook time: 10 minutes per batch | Serves 10 to 12

120 g plain flour
½ teaspoon baking powder
1 teaspoon salt
2 eggs, beaten
120 ml milk
2 tablespoons olive or vegetable

oil
185 g sliced almonds
900 g large prawns (about 32 to 40 prawns), peeled and deveined, tails left on
470 ml amaretto liqueur

1. Combine the flour, baking powder and salt in a large bowl. Add the eggs, milk and oil and stir until it forms a smooth batter. Coarsely crush the sliced almonds into a second shallow dish with your hands. 2. Dry the prawns well with paper towels. Dip the prawns into the batter and shake off any excess batter, leaving just enough to lightly coat the prawns. Transfer the prawns to the dish with the almonds and coat completely. Place the coated prawns on a plate or baking sheet and when all the prawns have been coated, freeze the prawns for an 1 hour, or as long as a week before air frying. 3. Preheat the air fryer to 204°C. 4. Transfer 8 frozen prawns at a time to the air fryer basket. Cook for 6 minutes. Turn the prawns over and cook for an additional 4 minutes. Repeat with the remaining prawns. 5. While the prawns are cooking, bring the Amaretto to a boil in a small saucepan on the stovetop. Lower the heat and simmer until it has reduced and thickened into a glaze, about 10 minutes. 6. Remove the prawns from the air fryer and brush both sides with the warm amaretto glaze. Serve warm.

Country Prawns

Prep time: 10 minutes | Cook time: 15 to 20 minutes | Serves 4

455 g large prawns, peeled and deveined, with tails on
455 g smoked sausage, cut into thick slices
2 corn cobs, quartered
1 courgette, cut into bite-sized pieces
1 red bell pepper, cut into chunks
1 tablespoon Old Bay seasoning
2 tablespoons olive oil
Cooking spray

1. Preheat the air fryer to 204ºC. Spray the air fryer basket lightly with cooking spray. 2. In a large bowl, mix the prawns, sausage, corn, courgette, bell pepper, and Old Bay seasoning, and toss to coat with the spices. Add the olive oil and toss again until evenly coated. 3. Spread the mixture in the air fryer basket in a single layer. You will need to cook in batches. 4. Cook for 15 to 20 minutes, or until cooked through, shaking the basket every 5 minutes for even cooking. 5. Serve immediately.

Air Fryer Fish Fry

Prep time: 5 minutes | Cook time: 15 minutes | Serves 4

470 ml low-fat buttermilk
½ teaspoon garlic powder
½ teaspoon onion powder
4 (110 g) sole fillets
70 g plain yellow cornmeal
45 g chickpea flour
¼ teaspoon cayenne pepper
Freshly ground black pepper

1. In a large bowl, combine the buttermilk, garlic powder, and onion powder. 2. Add the sole, turning until well coated, and set aside to marinate for 20 minutes. 3. In a shallow bowl, stir the cornmeal, chickpea flour, cayenne, and pepper together. 4. Dredge the fillets in the meal mixture, turning until well coated. Place in the basket of an air fryer. 5. Set the air fryer to 192ºC, close, and cook for 12 minutes.

Prawns with Swiss Chard

Prep time: 10 minutes | Cook time: 10 minutes | Serves 4

455 g prawns, peeled and deveined
½ teaspoon smoked paprika
70 g Swiss chard, chopped
2 tablespoons apple cider vinegar
1 tablespoon coconut oil
60 ml heavy cream

1. Mix prawns with smoked paprika and apple cider vinegar. 2. Put the prawns in the air fryer and add coconut oil. 3. Cook the prawns at 176ºC for 10 minutes. 4. Then mix cooked prawns with remaining ingredients and carefully mix.

Sesame-Crusted Tuna Steak

Prep time: 5 minutes | Cook time: 8 minutes | Serves 2

2 tuna steaks, 170 g each
1 tablespoon coconut oil, melted
½ teaspoon garlic powder
2 teaspoons white sesame seeds
2 teaspoons black sesame seeds

1. Brush each tuna steak with coconut oil and sprinkle with garlic powder. 2. In a large bowl, mix sesame seeds and then press each tuna steak into them, covering the steak as completely as possible. Place tuna steaks into the air fryer basket. 3. Adjust the temperature to 204ºC and cook for 8 minutes. 4. Flip the steaks halfway through the cooking time. Steaks will be well-done at 64ºC internal temperature. Serve warm.

Honey-Glazed Salmon

Prep time: 5 minutes | Cook time: 12 minutes | Serves 4

60 ml raw honey
4 garlic cloves, minced
1 tablespoon olive oil
½ teaspoon salt
Olive oil cooking spray
4 (1½-inch-thick) salmon fillets

1. Preheat the air fryer to 192ºC. 2. In a small bowl, mix together the honey, garlic, olive oil, and salt. 3. Spray the bottom of the air fryer basket with olive oil cooking spray, and place the salmon in a single layer on the bottom of the air fryer basket. 4. Brush the top of each fillet with the honey-garlic mixture, and cook for 10 to 12 minutes, or until the internal temperature reaches 64ºC.

Herbed Prawns Pita

Prep time: 5 minutes | Cook time: 8 minutes | Serves 4

455 g medium prawns, peeled and deveined
2 tablespoons olive oil
1 teaspoon dried oregano
½ teaspoon dried thyme
½ teaspoon garlic powder
¼ teaspoon onion powder
½ teaspoon salt
¼ teaspoon black pepper
4 whole wheat pitas
110 g feta cheese, crumbled
75 g shredded lettuce
1 tomato, diced
45 g black olives, sliced
1 lemon

1. Preheat the oven to 192ºC. 2. In a medium bowl, combine the prawns with the olive oil, oregano, thyme, garlic powder, onion powder, salt, and black pepper. 3. Pour prawns in a single layer in the air fryer basket and cook for 6 to 8 minutes, or until cooked through. 4. Remove from the air fryer and divide into warmed pitas with feta, lettuce, tomato, olives, and a squeeze of lemon.

New Orleans-Style Crab Cakes

Prep time: 10 minutes | Cook time: 8 to 10 minutes | Serves 4

190 g bread crumbs
2 teaspoons Creole Seasoning
1 teaspoon dry mustard
1 teaspoon salt
1 teaspoon freshly ground black pepper

360 g crab meat
2 large eggs, beaten
1 teaspoon butter, melted
⅓ cup minced onion
Cooking spray
Tartar Sauce, for serving

1. Preheat the air fryer to 176°C. Line the air fryer basket with baking paper. 2. In a medium bowl, whisk the bread crumbs, Creole Seasoning, dry mustard, salt, and pepper until blended. Add the crab meat, eggs, butter, and onion. Stir until blended. Shape the crab mixture into 8 patties. 3. Place the crab cakes on the baking paper and spritz with oil. 4. Cook for 4 minutes. Flip the cakes, spritz them with oil, and cook for 4 to 6 minutes more until the outsides are firm and a fork inserted into the center comes out clean. Serve with the Tartar Sauce.

Tuna Patty Sliders

Prep time: 15 minutes | Cook time: 10 to 15 minutes | Serves 4

3 cans tuna, 140 g each, packed in water
40 g whole-wheat panko bread crumbs
50 g shredded Parmesan cheese

1 tablespoon Sriracha
¾ teaspoon black pepper
10 whole-wheat buns
Cooking spray

1. Preheat the air fryer to 176°C. 2. Spray the air fryer basket lightly with cooking spray. 3. In a medium bowl combine the tuna, bread crumbs, Parmesan cheese, Sriracha, and black pepper and stir to combine. 4. Form the mixture into 10 patties. 5. Place the patties in the air fryer basket in a single layer. Spray the patties lightly with cooking spray. You may need to cook them in batches. 6. Cook for 6 to 8 minutes. Turn the patties over and lightly spray with cooking spray. Cook until golden brown and crisp, another 4 to 7 more minutes. Serve warm.

Italian Tuna Roast

Prep time: 15 minutes | Cook time: 21 to 24 minutes | Serves 8

Cooking spray
1 tablespoon Italian seasoning
⅛ teaspoon ground black pepper
1 tablespoon extra-light olive

oil
1 teaspoon lemon juice
1 (900 g) tuna loin, 3 to 4 inches thick

1. Spray baking dish with cooking spray and place in air fryer basket. Preheat the air fryer to 200°C. 2. Mix together the Italian seasoning, pepper, oil, and lemon juice. 3. Using a dull table knife or butter knife, pierce top of tuna about every half inch: Insert knife into top of tuna cook and pierce almost all the way to the bottom. 4. Spoon oil mixture into each of the holes and use the knife to push seasonings into the tuna as deeply as possible. 5. Spread any remaining oil mixture on all outer surfaces of tuna. 6. Place tuna cook in baking dish and cook for 20 minutes. Check temperature with a meat thermometer. Cook for an additional 1 to 4 minutes or until temperature reaches 64°C. 7. Remove basket from the air fryer and let tuna sit in the basket for 10 minutes.

White Fish with Cauliflower

Prep time: 30 minutes | Cook time: 13 minutes | Serves 4

230 g cauliflower florets
½ teaspoon English mustard
2 tablespoons butter, room temperature
½ tablespoon cilantro, minced

2 tablespoons sour cream
340 g cooked white fish
Salt and freshly cracked black pepper, to taste

1. Boil the cauliflower until tender. Then, purée the cauliflower in your blender. Transfer to a mixing dish. 2. Now, stir in the fish, cilantro, salt, and black pepper. 3. Add the sour cream, English mustard, and butter; mix until everything's well incorporated. Using your hands, shape into patties. 4. Place in the refrigerator for about 2 hours. Cook for 13 minutes at 202°C. Serve with some extra English mustard.

Paprika Crab Burgers

Prep time: 30 minutes | Cook time: 14 minutes | Serves 3

2 eggs, beaten
1 shallot, chopped
2 garlic cloves, crushed
1 tablespoon olive oil
1 teaspoon yellow mustard
1 teaspoon fresh coriander,

chopped
280 g crab meat
1 teaspoon smoked paprika
½ teaspoon ground black pepper
Sea salt, to taste
70 g Parmesan cheese

1. In a mixing bowl, thoroughly combine the eggs, shallot, garlic, olive oil, mustard, coriander, crab meat, paprika, black pepper, and salt. Mix until well combined. 2. Shape the mixture into 6 patties. Roll the crab patties over grated Parmesan cheese, coating well on all sides. Place in your refrigerator for 2 hours. 3. Spritz the crab patties with cooking oil on both sides. Cook in the preheated air fryer at 182°C for 14 minutes. Serve on dinner rolls if desired. Bon appétit!

Bacon-Wrapped Scallops

Prep time: 5 minutes | Cook time: 10 minutes | Serves 4

8 sea scallops, 30 g each, cleaned and patted dry
8 slices bacon

¼ teaspoon salt
¼ teaspoon ground black pepper

1. Wrap each scallop in 1 slice bacon and secure with a toothpick. Sprinkle with salt and pepper. 2. Place scallops into ungreased air fryer basket. Adjust the temperature to 182°C and cook for 10 minutes. Scallops will be opaque and firm, and have an internal temperature of 56°C when done. Serve warm.

Garlicky Cod Fillets

Prep time: 10 minutes | Cook time: 10 to 12 minutes | Serves 4

1 teaspoon olive oil
4 cod fillets
¼ teaspoon fine sea salt
¼ teaspoon ground black pepper, or more to taste
1 teaspoon cayenne pepper
8 g fresh Italian parsley,

coarsely chopped
120 ml milk
1 Italian pepper, chopped
4 garlic cloves, minced
1 teaspoon dried basil
½ teaspoon dried oregano

1. Lightly coat the sides and bottom of a baking dish with the olive oil. Set aside. 2. In a large bowl, sprinkle the fillets with salt, black pepper, and cayenne pepper. 3. In a food processor, pulse the remaining ingredients until smoothly puréed. 4. Add the purée to the bowl of fillets and toss to coat, then transfer to the prepared baking dish. 5. Preheat the air fryer to 192°C. 6. Put the baking dish in the air fryer basket and cook for 10 to 12 minutes, or until the fish flakes when pressed lightly with a fork. 7. Remove from the basket and serve warm.

Crab Cakes

Prep time: 10 minutes | Cook time: 10 minutes | Serves 4

2 cans lump crab meat, 170 g each
¼ cup blanched finely ground almond flour
1 large egg
2 tablespoons full-fat mayonnaise

½ teaspoon Dijon mustard
½ tablespoon lemon juice
½ medium green bell pepper, seeded and chopped
235 g chopped spring onion
½ teaspoon Old Bay seasoning

1. In a large bowl, combine all ingredients. Form into four balls and flatten into patties. Place patties into the air fryer basket. 2. Adjust the temperature to 176°C and cook for 10 minutes. 3. Flip patties halfway through the cooking time. Serve warm.

Miso Salmon

Prep time: 10 minutes | Cook time: 12 minutes | Serves 2

2 tablespoons brown sugar
2 tablespoons soy sauce
2 tablespoons white miso paste
1 teaspoon minced garlic
1 teaspoon minced fresh ginger
½ teaspoon freshly cracked

black pepper
2 salmon fillets, 140 g each
Vegetable oil spray
1 teaspoon sesame seeds
2 spring onions, thinly sliced, for garnish

1. In a small bowl, whisk together the brown sugar, soy sauce, miso, garlic, ginger, and pepper to combine. 2. Place the salmon fillets on a plate. Pour half the sauce over the fillets; turn the fillets to coat the other sides with sauce. 3. Spray the air fryer basket with vegetable oil spray. Place the sauce-covered salmon in the basket. Set the air fryer to 201°C for 12 minutes. Halfway through the cooking time, brush additional miso sauce on the salmon. 4. Sprinkle the salmon with the sesame seeds and spring onions and serve.

Sea Bass with Avocado Cream

Prep time: 30 minutes | Cook time: 9 minutes | Serves 4

Fish Fillets:
1½ tablespoons balsamic vinegar
120 ml vegetable broth
⅓ teaspoon shallot powder
1 tablespoon coconut aminos, or tamari
4 Sea Bass fillets
1 teaspoon ground black pepper
1½ tablespoons olive oil
Fine sea salt, to taste
⅓ teaspoon garlic powder

Avocado Cream:
2 tablespoons Greek-style yogurt
1 clove garlic, peeled and minced
1 teaspoon ground black pepper
½ tablespoon olive oil
80 ml vegetable broth
1 avocado
½ teaspoon lime juice
⅓ teaspoon fine sea salt

1. In a bowl, wash and pat the fillets dry using some paper towels. Add all the seasonings. In another bowl, stir in the remaining ingredients for the fish fillets. 2. Add the seasoned fish fillets; cover and let the fillets marinate in your refrigerator at least 3 hours. 3. Then, set the air fryer to 164°C. Cook marinated sea bass fillets in the air fryer grill basket for 9 minutes. 4. In the meantime, prepare the avocado sauce by mixing all the ingredients with an immersion blender or regular blender. Serve the sea bass fillets topped with the avocado sauce. Enjoy!

Panko Crab Sticks with Mayo Sauce

Prep time: 5 minutes | Cook time: 12 minutes | Serves 4

Crab Sticks:
2 eggs
120 g plain flour
50 g panko bread crumbs
1 tablespoon Old Bay seasoning
455 g crab sticks

Cooking spray
Mayo Sauce:
115 g mayonnaise
1 lime, juiced
2 garlic cloves, minced

1. Preheat air fryer to 200°C. 2. In a bowl, beat the eggs. In a shallow bowl, place the flour. In another shallow bowl, thoroughly combine the panko bread crumbs and old bay seasoning. 3. Dredge the crab sticks in the flour, shaking off any excess, then in the beaten eggs, finally press them in the bread crumb mixture to coat well. 4. Arrange the crab sticks in the air fryer basket and spray with cooking spray. 5. Cook for 12 minutes until golden brown. Flip the crab sticks halfway through the cooking time. 6. Meanwhile, make the sauce by whisking together the mayo, lime juice, and garlic in a small bowl. 7. Serve the crab sticks with the mayo sauce on the side.

Chapter 8 Desserts

Chocolate Soufflés

Prep time: 5 minutes | Cook time: 14 minutes | Serves 2

Butter and sugar for greasing the ramekins
85 g semi-sweet chocolate, chopped
55 g unsalted butter
2 eggs, yolks and white separated

3 tablespoons granulated sugar
½ teaspoon pure vanilla extract
2 tablespoons plain flour
Icing sugar, for dusting the finished soufflés
Heavy cream, for serving

1. Butter and sugar two 6-ounce (170 g) ramekins. (Butter the ramekins and then coat the butter with sugar by shaking it around in the ramekin and dumping out any excess.) 2. Melt the chocolate and butter together, either in the microwave or in a double boiler. In a separate bowl, beat the egg yolks vigorously. Add the sugar and the vanilla extract and beat well again. Drizzle in the chocolate and butter, mixing well. Stir in the flour, combining until there are no lumps. 3. Preheat the air fryer to 164°C. 4. In a separate bowl, whisk the egg whites to soft peak stage (the point at which the whites can almost stand up on the end of your whisk). Fold the whipped egg whites into the chocolate mixture gently and in stages. 5. Transfer the batter carefully to the buttered ramekins, leaving about ½-inch at the top. (You may have a little extra batter, depending on how airy the batter is, so you might be able to squeeze out a third soufflé if you want to.) Place the ramekins into the air fryer basket and cook for 14 minutes. The soufflés should have risen nicely and be brown on top. (Don't worry if the top gets a little dark, you'll be covering it with icing sugar in the next step.) 6. Dust with icing sugar and serve immediately with heavy cream to pour over the top at the table.

Blueberry Cream Cheese Bread Pudding

Prep time: 15 minutes | Cook time: 1 hour 10 minutes | Serves 6

240 ml single cream
4 large eggs
65 g granulated sugar, plus 3 tablespoons
1 teaspoon pure lemon extract

4 to 5 croissants, cubed
150 g blueberries
110 g cream cheese, cut into small cubes

1. In a large bowl, combine the cream, eggs, 65 g of sugar, and the extract. Whisk until well combined. Add the cubed croissants, blueberries, and cream cheese. Toss gently until everything is

thoroughly combined; set aside. 2. Place a 3-cup Bundt pan (a tube or Angel Food cake pan would work too) in the air fryer basket. Preheat the air fryer to 204°C. 3. Sprinkle the remaining 3 tablespoons sugar in the bottom of the hot pan. Cook for 10 minutes, or until the sugar caramelizes. Tip the pan to spread the caramel evenly across the bottom of the pan. 4. Remove the pan from the air fryer and pour in the bread mixture, distributing it evenly across the pan. Place the pan in the air fryer basket. Set the air fryer to 176°C and cook for 60 minutes, or until the custard is set in the middle. Let stand for 10 minutes before unmolding onto a serving plate.

Maple-Pecan Tart with Sea Salt

Prep time: 15 minutes | Cook time: 25 minutes | Serves 8

Tart Crust:
Vegetable oil spray
75 g unsalted butter, softened
50 g firmly packed brown sugar
125 g plain flour
¼ teaspoon kosher, or coarse sea salt
Filling:

4 tablespoons unsalted butter, diced
95 g packed brown sugar
60 ml pure maple syrup
60 ml whole milk
¼ teaspoon pure vanilla extract
190 g finely chopped pecans
¼ teaspoon flaked sea salt

1. For the crust: Line a baking pan with foil, leaving a couple of inches of overhang. Spray the foil with vegetable oil spray. 2. In a medium bowl, combine the butter and brown sugar. Beat with an electric mixer on medium-low speed until light and fluffy. Add the flour and kosher salt and beat until the ingredients are well blended. Transfer the mixture (it will be crumbly) to the prepared pan. Press it evenly into the bottom of the pan. 3. Place the pan in the air fryer basket. Set the air fryer to 176°C and cook for 13 minutes. When the crust has 5 minutes left to cook, start the filling. 4. For the filling: In a medium saucepan, combine the butter, brown sugar, maple syrup, and milk. Bring to a simmer, stirring occasionally. When it begins simmering, cook for 1 minute. Remove from the heat and stir in the vanilla and pecans. 5. Carefully pour the filling evenly over the crust, gently spreading with a rubber spatula so the nuts and liquid are evenly distributed. Keep the air fryer at 176°C and cook for 12 minutes, or until mixture is bubbling. (The center should still be slightly jiggly; it will thicken as it cools.) 6. Remove the pan from the air fryer and sprinkle the tart with the sea salt. Cool completely on a wire rack until room temperature. 7. Transfer the pan to the refrigerator to chill. When cold (the tart will be easier to cut), use the foil overhang to remove the tart from the pan and cut into 8 wedges. Serve at room temperature.

Orange, Anise & Ginger Skillet Cookie

Prep time: 20 minutes | Cook time: 15 minutes | Serves 2 to 4

Cookie:
Vegetable oil
125 g plain flour, plus 2 tablespoons
1 tablespoon grated orange zest
1 teaspoon ground ginger
1 teaspoon aniseeds, crushed
¼ teaspoon kosher, or coarse sea salt

4 tablespoons unsalted butter, at room temperature
100 g granulated sugar, plus more for sprinkling
3 tablespoons black treacle
1 large egg
Icing:
60 g icing sugar
2 to 3 teaspoons milk

1. For the cookie: Generously grease a baking pan with vegetable oil. 2. In a medium bowl, whisk together the flour, orange zest, ginger, aniseeds, and salt. 3. In a medium bowl using a hand mixer, beat the butter and sugar on medium-high speed until well combined, about 2 minutes. Add the treacle and egg and beat until light in color, about 2 minutes. Add the flour mixture and mix on low until just combined. Use a rubber spatula to scrape the dough into the prepared pan, spreading it to the edges and smoothing the top. Sprinkle with sugar. 4. Place the pan in the basket. Set the air fryer to 164°C and cook for 15 minutes, or until sides are browned but the center is still quite soft. 5. Let cool in the pan on a wire rack for 15 minutes. Turn the cookie out of the pan onto the rack. 6. For the icing: Whisk together the sugar and 2 teaspoons of milk. Add 1 teaspoon milk if needed for the desired consistency. Spread, or drizzle onto the cookie.

Brown Sugar Banana Bread

Prep time: 20 minutes | Cook time: 22 to 24 minutes | Serves 4

195 g packed light brown sugar
1 large egg, beaten
2 tablespoons unsalted butter, melted
120 ml milk, whole or semi-skimmed
250 g plain flour

1½ teaspoons baking powder
1 teaspoon ground cinnamon
½ teaspoon salt
1 banana, mashed
1 to 2 tablespoons coconut, or avocado oil oil
30 g icing sugar (optional)

1. In a large bowl, stir together the brown sugar, egg, melted butter, and milk. 2. In a medium bowl, whisk the flour, baking powder, cinnamon, and salt until blended. Add the flour mixture to the sugar mixture and stir just to blend. 3. Add the mashed banana and stir to combine. 4. Preheat the air fryer to 176°C. Spritz 2 mini loaf pans with oil. 5. Evenly divide the batter between the prepared pans and place them in the air fryer basket. 6. Cook for 22 to 24 minutes, or until a knife inserted into the middle of the loaves comes out clean. 7. Dust the warm loaves with icing sugar (if using).

Strawberry Scone Shortcake

Prep time: 10 minutes | Cook time: 20 minutes | Serves 4 to 6

165 g plain flour
3 tablespoons granulated sugar
1½ teaspoons baking powder
1 teaspoon kosher, or coarse sea salt
8 tablespoons unsalted butter, cubed and chilled
315 ml heavy cream, chilled

Turbinado (raw cane) sugar, for sprinkling
2 tablespoons icing sugar, plus more for dusting
½ teaspoon vanilla extract
165 g quartered fresh strawberries

1. In a large bowl, whisk together the flour, granulated sugar, baking powder, and salt. Add the butter and use your fingers to break apart the butter pieces while working them into the flour mixture, until pea-size pieces form. Pour 155 ml of the cream over the flour mixture and, using a rubber spatula, mix the ingredients together until just combined. 2. Transfer the dough to a work surface and form into a 7 inch wide disk. Brush the top with water, then sprinkle with some turbinado sugar. Using a large metal spatula, transfer the dough to the air fryer and cook at 176°C until golden brown and fluffy, about 20 minutes. Let cool in the air fryer basket for 5 minutes, then turn out onto a wire rack, right-side up, to cool completely. 3. Meanwhile, in a bowl, beat the remaining 155 ml of cream, the icing sugar, and vanilla until stiff peaks form. Split the scone like a hamburger bun and spread the strawberries over the bottom. Top with the whipped cream and cover with the top of the scone. Dust with icing sugar and cut into wedges to serve.

Funnel Cake

Prep time: 10 minutes | Cook time: 5 minutes | Serves 4

Coconut, or avocado oil, for spraying
110 g self-raising flour, plus more for dusting

240 ml fat-free vanilla Greek yogurt
½ teaspoon ground cinnamon
¼ cup icing sugar

1. Preheat the air fryer to 192°C. Line the air fryer basket with baking paper, and spray lightly with oil. 2. In a large bowl, mix together the flour, yogurt and cinnamon until the mixture forms a ball. 3. Place the dough on a lightly floured work surface and knead for about 2 minutes. 4. Cut the dough into 4 equal pieces, then cut each of those into 6 pieces. You should have 24 pieces in total. 5. Roll the pieces into 8- to 10-inch-long ropes. Loosely mound the ropes into 4 piles of 6 ropes. 6. Place the dough piles in the prepared basket, and spray liberally with oil. You may need to work in batches, depending on the size of your air fryer. 7. Cook for 5 minutes, or until lightly browned. 8. Dust with the icing sugar before serving.

Gluten-Free Spice Cookies

Prep time: 10 minutes | Cook time: 12 minutes | Serves 4

4 tablespoons unsalted butter, at room temperature	2 teaspoons ground ginger
2 tablespoons agave nectar	1 teaspoon ground cinnamon
1 large egg	½ teaspoon freshly grated nutmeg
2 tablespoons water	1 teaspoon baking soda
240 g almond flour	¼ teaspoon kosher, or coarse sea salt
100 g granulated sugar	

1. Line the bottom of the air fryer basket with baking paper cut to fit. 2. In a large bowl, using a hand mixer, beat together the butter, agave, egg, and water on medium speed until light and fluffy. 3. Add the almond flour, sugar, ginger, cinnamon, nutmeg, baking soda, and salt. Beat on low speed until well combined. 4. Roll the dough into 2-tablespoon balls and arrange them on the baking paper in the basket. (They don't really spread too much but try to leave a little room between them.) Set the air fryer to 164ºC, and cook for 12 minutes, or until the tops of cookies are lightly browned. 5. Transfer to a wire rack and let cool completely. Store in an airtight container for up to a week.

Pineapple Galette

Prep time: 15 minutes | Cook time: 40 minutes | Serves 2

¼ medium-size pineapple, peeled, cored, and cut crosswise into ¼-inch-thick slices	Finely grated zest of ½ lime
2 tablespoons dark rum, or apple juice	1 store-bought sheet puff pastry, cut into an 8-inch round
1 teaspoon vanilla extract	3 tablespoons granulated sugar
½ teaspoon kosher, or coarse sea salt	2 tablespoons unsalted butter, cubed and chilled
	Coconut ice cream, for serving

1. In a small bowl, combine the pineapple slices, rum, vanilla, salt, and lime zest and let stand for at least 10 minutes to allow the pineapple to soak in the rum. 2. Meanwhile, press the puff pastry round into the bottom and up the sides of a cake pan and use the tines of a fork to dock the bottom and sides. 3. Arrange the pineapple slices on the bottom of the pastry in a more or less single layer, then sprinkle with the sugar and dot with the butter. Drizzle with the leftover juices from the bowl. Place the pan in the air fryer and cook at 154ºC until the pastry is puffed and golden brown and the pineapple is lightly caramelized on top, about 40 minutes. 4. Transfer the pan to a wire rack to cool for 15 minutes. Unmold the galette from the pan and serve warm with coconut ice cream.

Old-Fashioned Fudge Pie

Prep time: 15 minutes | Cook time: 25 to 30 minutes | Serves 8

300 g granulated sugar	melted
40 g unsweetened cocoa powder	1½ teaspoons vanilla extract
70 g self-raising flour	1 (9-inch) unbaked piecrust
3 large eggs, unbeaten	30 g icing sugar (optional)
12 tablespoons unsalted butter,	

1. In a medium bowl, stir together the sugar, cocoa powder, and flour. Stir in the eggs and melted butter. Stir in the vanilla. 2. Preheat the air fryer to 176ºC. 3. Pour the chocolate filing into the crust. 4. Cook for 25 to 30 minutes, stirring every 10 minutes, until a knife inserted into the middle comes out clean. Let sit for 5 minutes before dusting with icing sugar (if using) to serve.

Mixed Berry Hand Pies

Prep time: 5 minutes | Cook time: 30 minutes | Serves 4

150 g granulated sugar	two equal portions
½ teaspoon ground cinnamon	1 teaspoon water
1 tablespoon cornflour	1 package refrigerated shortcrust pastry (or your own homemade pastry)
150 g blueberries	
150 g blackberries	
150 g raspberries, divided into	1 egg, beaten

1. Combine the sugar, cinnamon, and cornstarch in a small saucepan. Add the blueberries, blackberries, and ½ of the raspberries. Toss the berries gently to coat them evenly. Add the teaspoon of water to the saucepan and turn the stovetop on to medium-high heat, stirring occasionally. Once the berries break down, release their juice, and start to simmer (about 5 minutes), simmer for another couple of minutes and then transfer the mixture to a bowl, stir in the remaining ½ of the raspberries and let it cool. 2. Preheat the air fryer to 188ºC. 3. Cut the pie dough into four 5-inch circles and four 6-inch circles. 4. Spread the 6-inch circles on a flat surface. Divide the berry filling between all four circles. Brush the perimeter of the dough circles with a little water. Place the 5-inch circles on top of the filling and press the perimeter of the dough circles together to seal. Roll the edges of the bottom circle up over the top circle to make a crust around the filling. Press a fork around the crust to make decorative indentations and to seal the crust shut. Brush the pies with egg wash and sprinkle a little sugar on top. Poke a small hole in the center of each pie with a paring knife to vent the dough. 5. Cook two pies at a time. Brush or spray the air fryer basket with oil and place the pies into the basket. Cook for 9 minutes. Turn the pies over and cook for another 6 minutes. Serve warm or at room temperature.

Cardamom Custard

Prep time: 10 minutes | Cook time: 25 minutes | Serves 2

240 ml whole milk

1 large egg

2 tablespoons granulated sugar, plus 1 teaspoon

¼ teaspoon vanilla bean paste or pure vanilla extract

¼ teaspoon ground cardamom, plus more for sprinkling

1. In a medium bowl, beat together the milk, egg, sugar, vanilla, and cardamom. 2. Place two ramekins in the air fryer basket. Divide the mixture between the ramekins. Sprinkle lightly with cardamom. Cover each ramekin tightly with aluminum foil. Set the air fryer to 176ºC and cook for 25 minutes, or until a toothpick inserted in the center comes out clean. 3. Let the custards cool on a wire rack for 5 to 10 minutes. 4. Serve warm or refrigerate until cold and serve chilled.

Boston Cream Donut Holes

Prep time: 30 minutes | Cook time: 4 minutes per batch | Makes 24 donut holes

200 g bread flour

1 teaspoon active dry yeast

1 tablespoon granulated sugar

¼ teaspoon salt

120 ml warm milk

½ teaspoon pure vanilla extract

2 egg yolks

2 tablespoons unsalted butter, melted

Vegetable oil

Custard Filling:

95 g box French vanilla instant pudding mix

175 ml whole milk

60 ml heavy cream

Chocolate Glaze:

170 g chocolate chips

80 ml heavy cream

1. Combine the flour, yeast, sugar, and salt in the bowl of a stand mixer. Add the milk, vanilla, egg yolks and butter. Mix until the dough starts to come together in a ball. Transfer the dough to a floured surface and knead the dough by hand for 2 minutes. Shape the dough into a ball, place it in a large, oiled bowl, cover the bowl with a clean kitchen towel and let the dough rise for 1 to 1½ hours or until the dough has doubled in size. 2. When the dough has risen, punch it down and roll it into a 24-inch log. Cut the dough into 24 pieces and roll each piece into a ball. Place the dough balls on a baking sheet and let them rise for another 30 minutes. 3. Preheat the air fryer to 204ºC. 4. Spray or brush the dough balls lightly with vegetable oil and cook eight at a time for 4 minutes, turning them over halfway through the cooking time. 5. While donut holes are cooking, make the filling and chocolate glaze. Make the filling: Use an electric hand mixer to beat the French vanilla pudding, milk and ¼ cup of heavy cream together for 2 minutes. 6. Make the chocolate glaze: Place the chocolate chips in a medium-sized bowl. Bring the heavy cream to a boil on the stovetop and pour it over the chocolate chips. Stir until the chips are melted and the glaze is smooth. 7. To fill the donut holes, place the custard filling in a pastry bag with a long tip. Poke a hole into the side of the donut hole with a small knife. Wiggle the knife around to make room for the filling. Place the pastry bag tip into the hole and slowly squeeze the custard into the center of the donut. Dip the top half of the donut into the chocolate glaze, letting any excess glaze drip back into the bowl. Let the glazed donut holes sit for a few minutes before serving

Coconut Macaroons

Prep time: 5 minutes | Cook time: 8 to 10 minutes | Makes 12 macaroons

120 g desiccated, sweetened coconut

4½ teaspoons plain flour

2 tablespoons sugar

1 egg white

½ teaspoon almond extract

1. Preheat the air fryer to 164ºC. 2. In a medium bowl, mix all ingredients together. 3. Shape coconut mixture into 12 balls. 4. Place all 12 macaroons in air fryer basket. They won't expand, so you can place them close together, but they shouldn't touch. 5. Cook for 8 to 10 minutes, until golden.

Pumpkin-Spice Bread Pudding

Prep time: 15 minutes | Cook time: 35 minutes | Serves 6

Bread Pudding:

175 ml heavy whipping cream

120 g canned pumpkin

80 ml whole milk

65 g granulated sugar

1 large egg plus 1 yolk

½ teaspoon pumpkin pie spice

⅛ teaspoon kosher, or coarse sea salt

1/3 loaf of day-old baguette or crusty country bread, cubed

4 tablespoons unsalted butter, melted

Sauce:

80 ml pure maple syrup

1 tablespoon unsalted butter

120 ml heavy whipping cream

½ teaspoon pure vanilla extract

1. For the bread pudding: In a medium bowl, combine the cream, pumpkin, milk, sugar, egg and yolk, pumpkin pie spice, and salt. Whisk until well combined. 2. In a large bowl, toss the bread cubes with the melted butter. Add the pumpkin mixture and gently toss until the ingredients are well combined. 3. Transfer the mixture to a baking pan. Place the pan in the air fryer basket. Set the fryer to 176ºC cooking for 35 minutes, or until custard is set in the middle. 4. Meanwhile, for the sauce: In a small saucepan, combine the syrup and butter. Heat over medium heat, stirring, until the butter melts. Stir in the cream and simmer, stirring often, until the sauce has thickened, about 15 minutes. Stir in the vanilla. Remove the pudding from the air fryer. 5. Let the pudding stand for 10 minutes before serving with the warm sauce.

Molten Chocolate Almond Cakes

Prep time: 5 minutes | Cook time: 13 minutes | Serves 3

Butter and flour for the ramekins
110 g bittersweet chocolate, chopped
110 g unsalted butter
2 eggs
2 egg yolks
50 g granulated sugar
½ teaspoon pure vanilla extract, or almond extract

1 tablespoon plain flour
3 tablespoons ground almonds
8 to 12 semisweet chocolate discs (or 4 chunks of chocolate)
Cocoa powder or icing sugar, for dusting
Toasted almonds, coarsely chopped

1. Butter and flour three (170 g) ramekins. (Butter the ramekins and then coat the butter with flour by shaking it around in the ramekin and dumping out any excess.) 2. Melt the chocolate and butter together, either in the microwave or in a double boiler. In a separate bowl, beat the eggs, egg yolks and sugar together until light and smooth. Add the vanilla extract. Whisk the chocolate mixture into the egg mixture. Stir in the flour and ground almonds. 3. Preheat the air fryer to 164ºC. 4. Transfer the batter carefully to the buttered ramekins, filling halfway. Place two or three chocolate discs in the center of the batter and then fill the ramekins to ½-inch below the top with the remaining batter. Place the ramekins into the air fryer basket and cook for 13 minutes. The sides of the cake should be set, but the centers should be slightly soft. Remove the ramekins from the air fryer and let the cakes sit for 5 minutes. (If you'd like the cake a little less molten, cook for 14 minutes and let the cakes sit for 4 minutes.) 5. Run a butter knife around the edge of the ramekins and invert the cakes onto a plate. Lift the ramekin off the plate slowly and carefully so that the cake doesn't break. Dust with cocoa powder or icing sugar and serve with a scoop of ice cream and some coarsely chopped toasted almonds.

S'mores

Prep time: 5 minutes | Cook time: 30 seconds | Makes 8 s'mores

Coconut, or avocado oil, for spraying
8 digestive biscuits

2 (45 g) chocolate bars
4 large marshmallows

1. Line the air fryer basket with baking paper and spray lightly with oil. 2. Place 4 biscuits into the prepared basket. 3. Break the chocolate bars in half, and place 1/2 on top of each biscuit. Top with 1 marshmallow. 4. Cook at 188ºC for 30 seconds, or until the marshmallows are puffed, golden brown and slightly melted. 5. Top with the remaining biscuits and serve.

Ricotta Lemon Poppy Seed Cake

Prep time: 10 minutes | Cook time: 55 minutes | Serves 4

Unsalted butter, at room temperature
110 g almond flour
100 g granulated sugar
3 large eggs
55 g heavy cream
60 g full-fat ricotta cheese

55 g coconut oil, melted
2 tablespoons poppy seeds
1 teaspoon baking powder
1 teaspoon pure lemon extract
Grated zest and juice of 1 lemon, plus more zest for garnish

1. Generously butter a baking pan. Line the bottom of the pan with baking paper cut to fit. 2. In a large bowl, combine the almond flour, sugar, eggs, cream, ricotta, coconut oil, poppy seeds, baking powder, lemon extract, lemon zest, and lemon juice. Beat with a hand mixer on medium speed, until well blended and fluffy. 3. Pour the batter into the prepared pan. Cover the pan tightly with aluminum foil. Set the pan in the air fryer basket. Set the air fryer to 164ºC and cook for 45 minutes. Remove the foil and cook for 10 to 15 minutes more, until a knife (do not use a toothpick) inserted into the center of the cake comes out clean. 4. Let the cake cool in the pan on a wire rack for 10 minutes. Remove the cake from pan and let it cool on the rack for 15 minutes before slicing. 5. Top with additional lemon zest, slice and serve.

5-Ingredient Brownies

Prep time: 10 minutes | Cook time: 25 minutes | Serves 6

Vegetable oil
110 g unsalted butter
½ cup chocolate chips

3 large eggs
100 g granulated sugar
1 teaspoon pure vanilla extract

1. Generously grease a baking pan with vegetable oil. 2. In a microwave-safe bowl, combine the butter and chocolate chips. Microwave on high for 1 minute. Stir very well. (You want the heat from the butter and chocolate to melt the remaining clumps. If you microwave until everything melts, the chocolate will be overcooked. If necessary, microwave for an additional 10 seconds, but stir well before you try that.) 3. In a medium bowl, combine the eggs, sugar, and vanilla. Whisk until light and frothy. Whisking continuously, slowly pour in the melted chocolate in a thin stream and whisk until everything is incorporated. 4. Pour the batter into the prepared pan. Set the pan in the air fryer basket. Set the air fryer to 176ºC, and cook for 25 minutes, or until a toothpick inserted into the center comes out clean. 5. Let cool in the pan on a wire rack for 30 minutes before cutting into squares.

Grilled Pineapple Dessert

Prep time: 5 minutes | Cook time: 12 minutes | Serves 4

Coconut, or avocado oil for misting, or cooking spray

4½-inch-thick slices fresh pineapple, core removed

1 tablespoon honey

¼ teaspoon brandy, or apple juice

2 tablespoons slivered almonds, toasted

Vanilla frozen yogurt, coconut sorbet, or ice cream

1. Spray both sides of pineapple slices with oil or cooking spray. Place into air fryer basket. 2. Cook at 200°C for 6 minutes. Turn slices over and cook for an additional 6 minutes. 3. Mix together the honey and brandy. 4. Remove cooked pineapple slices from air fryer, sprinkle with toasted almonds, and drizzle with honey mixture. 5. Serve with a scoop of frozen yogurt or sorbet on the side.

Printed in Great Britain
by Amazon

12765583R00038